You Can Find It Wild

Selected Writings On
Maine's Natural Wonders

Florence L. Heyl

Edited by Mary Liz Heyl Bauer
Cover Photographs by Tom Fegely
Illustrations by D.D. Tyler

Published by Florence L. Heyl
East Boothbay, Maine

ISBN #9 781591 961222 5119

Cover Photographs ©2002 Tom Fegely

Top: Loon; Second Row: Rhododendron, Chipmunk, Saw Whet Owl
Third Row: Red Foxes; Fourth Row: Heron, Flying Squirrel

Illustrations:

Balsam fir: © 1992 Diana Dee Tyler; Cherries: © 2000 Diana Dee Tyler;
Chickadee: ©1992 Diana Dee Tyler; Goldfinches: © 2001 Diana Dee Tyler;
Geese: ©1994 Diana Dee Tyler; Hummingbird: ©2002 Diana Dee Tyler;
Indian pipes: ©1992 Diana Dee Tyler; Loon: ©1984 Diana Dee Tyler; Mink:
©1983 Diana Dee Tyler; Moose: ©1983 Diana Dee Tyler; Owl: ©1983 Diana
Dee Tyler; Porcupine: ©1983 Diana Dee Tyler; Raccoon: ©1979 Diana Dee
Tyler; Redfox: ©1993 Diana Dee Tyler; Skunk: ©1983 Diana Dee Tyler;
Starfish: ©1993 Diana Dee Tyler; Tadpoles: ©1995 Diana Dee Tyler;

Production Note: You Can Find It Wild was set in 12-point Triplex, an Emigre typeface
designed by Zuzana Licko in 1989. Printed by instantpublishers.com.

To **Mary J. Littlefield**, my camp director at

Camps Madeleine Mulford and Watchung (N.J.)

who awakened my interest in nature's wonders.

ACKNOWLEDGEMENTS

I give special thanks to all who helped to make this publication possible: to Edward Miller, who as editor of the *Call Chronicle* in Allentown, Pa. (now the *Morning Call*) first accepted my column in 1970 providing me with my start in this very rewarding adventure; to Mary Brewer, editor of the *Boothbay Register* and to Abbie Roberts, editor of *The Lincoln County News*, who both provided encouragement and support throughout the 25+ years of publications; to my husband, John, who explored ponds and woodlands with me; to Tom Fegely for his nature photographs and his friendship and support over the years; to D.D. Tyler, a Maine artist of natural history, for use of her wonderful illustrations; to Peggy Voight for her original assistance in preparing material for presentation to publishers; to Deborah Heppner Bozes who typed the selected articles from faded, worn copies; to my son-in-law, Bob Bauer, and Louise Sanderson who were diligent proof readers; to my grandson, Jeff Bauer, for marketing my book on the internet; to Cheryl Gregory for scanning the illustrations; to Gayle F. Hendricks who provided the design and technological expertise essential to bring this project to fruition and to my daughter, Mary Liz, who made the final selections and edited this publication.

EDITOR'S NOTES

When my mother, Florence L. Heyl, began her weekly nature column in the *Call-Chronicle* newspaper (Allentown, Pa.—now *The Morning Call*) in 1970, she told me that she hoped to encourage the public to be more aware of the natural beauties around them. Each week she would choose a nature topic that anyone out for a walk in a park, woodland area, or observing the natural activities in their backyard could easily find and and learn more about. She felt that as more people appreciated the wonders of the natural world, they would also become advocates for preserving the environment.

Over the more than 30 years that my mother wrote her column *You Can Find It Wild* for the *Call-Chronicle* (1970-74) and for the *Boothbay Register* and *The Lincoln County News* in Maine (1973-2002), I think she achieved her goal. Drawing from her own knowledge and extensive collection of resource materials, she produced her weekly column on her small manual typewriter. In both locations, she received fan letters and phone calls with praise and questions about what her readers had observed. She treated each request with interest and enthusiasm and responded personally to each one.

It is with great pleasure that I am able to share with you a selection of her columns that were published in the *Boothbay Register* and *The Lincoln County News* between 1973 and 2002.

I chose a variety for each season, trying to have a representation of birds, mammals, and plant life. I included articles that dealt with her joy of sharing her love of nature with family and friends, since that was always one of her major motivations.

I hope this collection will inspire you to observe and love the natural wonders around us and to share your appreciation with others, especially the young people in your lives. Nothing would please my mother more!

—*Mary Liz Heyl Bauer*

TABLE OF CONTENTS

AUTUMN

WINTER

S P R I N G

I think there is no other thing

to match the willow in the spring!

—Bertha E. Jaques

AWAKENINGS

"February is done and gone. March has arrived at last. And whether it came in like a lion or a lamb, one thing is sure: already, in a host of bloodstreams and sap streams and woodland streams, spring is surging upward and outward. You can bet on it—just as sure as you can bet on sunrise tomorrow. One minute earlier than today."

That's the way Ronald Rood concludes the chapter entitled "First Call" in his book, *Who Wakes the Groundhog?* (Norton)

We've already heard the chickadee's spring "fee-bee" call. Have you? You begin to notice some flirting among our year-round resident birds—the nuthatches, cardinals, woodpeckers, chickadees, and titmice. Nothing serious, yet. Just flirting —but the behavior lets us know which is the male and which is the female! A male cardinal or nuthatch may even husk a sunflower seed for that pretty little female who had managed very well without him all winter long. Mourning doves sit close together on a pine bough, cooing and billing. These will be the first of the songbirds to actually get down to the business of nesting, and they may raise several broods before autumn.

But for most of the raptorial birds—hawks and owls—the nesting season begins still earlier. For the great-horned owl and for the bald eagle, for instance, pairing is already settled and the nesting site decided upon. By late March of last year (1982) the bald eagles at Damariscotta Lake were incubating eggs. Great-horned owls may even have owlets by this time. It is important for these predatory birds to get an early start. In the case of the bald eagle, the eggs require from five to six weeks incubation and the young birds do not even leave the nest until ten to eleven weeks after hatching. The eggs of the great-horned owls must be incubated for almost as long (four-and-a-half to five weeks) and the young birds, although they leave the nest at about five weeks after hatching, do not fly well for another five weeks. They depend upon their parents for food over a still longer period. So if the eaglets and the owlets are to be self-sufficient adults by summer's end, the breeding season must get an early start. By the time these young birds have hatched and need a lot of food, there will be an abundance of it for them. Wood mice, meadow voles, and shrews are venturing out from their under snow labyrinths and they're apt to be careless. Rabbits frolic together—until one of them is snatched to provide dinner for a nestful of young birds.

Some of the mammals have already given birth, black bears, for instance. This is the mating time for skunks, raccoons, and red squirrels. The gray squirrel female is probably already pregnant.

So much for the bloodstreams' responses to the upward and outward surging of spring.

Ronald Rood referred to sap streams. It's that time of year when buckets hang on sugar maple trees, reminding us that the "sap's runnin'." There are plenty of other reminders. Tree buds are swollen and some trees take on more color—red maple and the willows, for instance. Those who thought of it and who could tramp through the snow of two weeks ago could by now have forsythia forced into showing golden color. Pussy willow is ready for clipping, too.

And as the snow and frost melts, the woodland streams become full and musical—or downright noisy—and the insect and amphibious and fish life become active.

Some species of animal life are absolutely dependent upon proper timing if they are to survive. A ruby-throated hummingbird should not arrive at its summer territory until there is nectar ready for the sipping. The eggs of the praying mantis, massed in a coating of hardened bubbles, should not hatch until there are live insects to be eaten. Caterpillars should not break through their egg shells until there are soft new leaves for them to chew.

Sometimes signals are not received. In 1974, scarlet tanagers, having wintered in tropical South America, arrived in northern Maine in the third week of May as usual—without having received the message that Maine and all of northern New England were experiencing a very late spring. Tree swallows had arrived a few days earlier. We were at Kidney Pond in Baxter Park that week and it was pathetic to see the dying birds on the ground. Trees were not yet leafed out; therefore leaf-eating insects had not hatched and there was no food for the tanagers. Tree swallows were having a rough time of it, too. There were no mosquitoes or black flies to bother us— nor to be devoured by the swallows. Warblers of various species sought flowering trees, red maple especially, where we suppose they found insects attracted by the pollen. We have, in another cold May, seen a kingbird at Sourdnekunk Field, hopping on the ground and looking quite miserable. He might have obtained an occasional insect among the dry grass—but he should have been catching flies "on the wing".

Some species are more omnivorous and can adjust their eating habits. The fox would prefer a rabbit, but a mouse or even dried berries will do. In February, a flock of approximately twenty robins were seen feeding at low tide at Spruce Point. These are certainly not seafood-eating birds—but where could they find worms? Berries? A few, but withering and probably tasteless. The robins adapted and found rich protein food at the tide's edge.

So we see that these weeks of late winter and early spring are exciting and important ones for wildlife. They are fraught with danger for all wild creatures, yet they are the weeks that offer them the greatest opportunity for life's fulfillment.

Mach 3, 1983

A PRICKLY PACIFIST

If there is a porcupine in the neighborhood, this is the season when we are likely to know it. A few weeks ago, when looking for the great gray owl reported in West Boothbay Harbor, friends and I noted that one side of a tree—a red maple, I think—was stripped of its bark. A knowledgeable naturalist remarked, "That's the work of a porcupine." Last spring while snow still lay on the woodland trail leading to Morse Mountain (near Phippsburg), a group of us observed how porcupines had bared the trunks of a small grove of trees. You could tell how deep the snow had been by noting the height of the intact bark. It's just about a year ago that John and I saw a "porky" which had been killed on Route 96 in East Boothbay. He had been lured there by the salt, which he craves. In fact, he craves it so much that he will chew the handle of a canoe paddle or axe, or any other item that is impregnated with sweat.

In these ways—damaging of trees and campers' gear—this large, clumsy rodent makes himself unwelcome, even obnoxious, around human habitation. Then, too, he is feared because of his quills. That the quills are effective weapons, there is no doubt. However, the common belief that he can "shoot" them is false. There must be direct contact and, actually, the porcupine is by nature a peaceable fellow, asking only not to be molested.

Although earlier confused with "prickly beasts" of the Old World, such as the hedgehog of Europe and the crested porcupine of Africa which is a burrowing animal, our porcupine, an arboreal rodent, is strictly a member of the western world. It evolved in South America which for some 70 million years was separated from North America. The land bridge between the two continents was restored about 5 million years ago and mammals were then able to expand their territories from the south into the north and vice versa. Two

4

species of porcupines—*erethizon dorsatum* and *erethizon coendou*—did move northward. Only *E. dorsatum* came as far as the U.S. and by now this *porcus-pinnae* or "spined pig" (which is not a pig at all, of course) is quite at home in nearly all forested areas of North America, including most of Canada and even into Labrador and Alaska. In fact, although in far distant times our U.S. porky was a mammal of a warm even hot climate, he now shows a distinct preference for a cool climate with "real" winters.

Call him—consider him—stupid, clumsy, lazy, if you choose. He is. Or call him, as a species, exceedingly clever in the ways in which he has solved the problems, met the needs, common to all mammals, including ourselves—those of food, shelter, defense, propagation. Take food. He's a vegetarian and can eat almost anything that grows. He enjoys cow lily and water lily and lush green shoots in their season but he also likes the inner bark of northern trees—beech, poplar, birch, and all of the evergreens, especially hemlock. And he is well equipped for tree-climbing, with sharp claws and a strong tail which serves as a brace. Warm and snug in his 3-inch-thick fur pelt, he can stay aloft through a severe blizzard, sleeping when he needs to, eating the bark within his easy reach when he's hungry. He builds no house as does the beaver, and he does not need to spend energy by run-

ning from danger as do deer and many other creatures. That's because he's so well armored.

The quills (some 30,000 on a fully equipped adult) are normally held low and relaxed, beneath the fur. Long guard-hairs extend beyond the fur and serve to alert the porcupine to danger, instantly triggering the erection of the quills. The fisher is the one wild creature that has learned how to subdue the porcupine upon whose meat he likes to dine! Other predatory animals are seldom successful. Veterinarians have removed many quills from adventurous or foolish dogs. Great horned owls, having sought food for hungry owlets in the springtime, have been found dead with several quills in their heads. Coyotes, bobcats, wolves, and lynxes are among the mammals slain by porcupine quills which are barbed and inflict wounds which become readily infected. Yet, he cannot "shoot" them and actually prefers not to use them at all. Sometimes called "a prickly pacifist", he'd rather not fight. Alarmed, he heads into the nearest corner such as tree roots and raises his tail in warning. If his adversary advances, contacting the porcupine, he is pierced with the painful barbs. Or the porcupine, if enough provoked, will back into his foe with the same result. The porcupine may thrash his tail against the enemy or against a wall. The quills are readily released, falling to the ground or penetrating the victim's hide—but they are not propelled.

So we see that the porcupine has simplified his needs of food and shelter and defense. With a good survival rate it is not necessary for this mammal to be prolific. One infant per year suffices to keep the population stable and that young one is born with its eyes open, well-furred, with spines that are firm soon after birth. He can climb, swim, and chew vegetable material almost immediately, so there is a very short nursing time. Mother porcupine keeps her child close by during most of its first year—to show him the trails and the good trees and to teach him what he'll need to know—but her actual duties are minimal. Thus the porcupine has simplified the propagation problem, also!

For very good further reading I recommend Jack Schaefer's *Animal Bestiary* and *Aloysius the Independent* by William D. Berry in *The Audubon Book of True Nature Stores*, edited by John K. Terres, and the write-up on the porcupine in *The Imperial Collection of Audubon Animals* by John James Audubon and John Bachman. They're all excellent.

March 8, 1979

THE HERON FAMILY

When we look at a map of Maine we see that a large proportion of it is colored blue, indicating water. Even so, it's a surprise to learn that of the 12 members of the heron family native to North America ten are seen in our own state during the warm months, some of them from early April until October. One of them, the handsome great blue heron, is sometimes reported as overwintering here. Of these ten species all but the great or "common" egret and the yellow-crowned night heron also breed in Maine.

So today we'll pay special attention to our herons and we'll focus first on the great blue because it's the heron whose habits and haunts provide us the best opportunities to observe him. We see him from cruise boats and also from a car. A few days ago we saw three great blues feeding in pools of water left by a receding tide. We had turned off Route One in Edgecomb's Muddy Rudder, taking the back road to Route 96. At low tide we see the tall wader in mud flats and on rock-weed covered ledges, and along the shores of freshwater lakes and rivers. At such times he's apt to be a loner, standing motionless but tensely poised, waiting for the precise moment to plunge the strong yellow bill into the water to secure a fish. And we've seen this large heron flying across the water with slow, steady wing-beats, neck folded, crooked into an S, and legs stretched straight out behind.

Maine's other herons include the green, the little blue, the great and the snowy egrets, the Louisiana heron, the black-crowned and the yellow-crowned herons, and the American and least bitterns. In addition, we have the cattle egret which is "self-introduced" from Eurasia and Africa. This one is the maverick, preferring a diet of field insects which they secure most easily when the insects have been disturbed by grazing cows and horses. Although we think of fish as the primary food of the other herons, there are actually large quantities of aquatic insects and amphibians consumed by the waders. Crayfish, salamanders, frogs and tadpoles, moths, water beetles, shrimp, crabs, as well as mice and shrews, even the swift dragonflies become the prey of herons, serving, along with small fish, to nourish these beautiful birds.

All herons fly in the same manner as the great blues. Most have long necks and long legs. The bill, although the color and relative length may vary with the species, is always straight and strong, almost daggerlike.

But there are differences between these members of the heron family. Those that are called "egret" have beautiful, long, nuptial plumes which were known earlier as "aigrettes." These were so avidly sought by milliners for decorating women's hats that the craze almost caused the extinction of the egrets but instead led to their protection. Most egrets are white and, like most herons, they have exceptionally long, slender legs—necessary for wading. Usually they feed out in the open.

Although egrets and those called herons are quite noticeable if nearby, the bitterns are masters at concealment. They stand among cattails and marsh grasses where their streaked breasts blend with the vertical lines all around them, resulting in very effective camouflage. You can paddle your canoe right past him without detecting his presence. If truly alarmed the bittern takes off clumsily, with a hoarse squawk. These herons have somewhat shorter legs and stockier bodies than those of the tall waders.

Each of these birds has its distinguishing features. The snowy egret has "golden slippers," the great egret has "black stockings" and a yellow bill. The bitternlike green heron has an iridescent blue-green back and a dark, shaggy crest.

Wouldn't it be a challenging project to see all of Maine's herons (ten native; plus the cattle egret) during this spring-through-autumn period? It will be challenging, yes, but quite achievable. Except for the bitterns they are usually observable at a comfortable level and if you study the heron section of the *Peterson Field Guide* you can readily identify the species. Also, a heron usually "stays put" long enough for you to check it out. Best of all, it's apt to be found just where we ourselves would like to be in the summertime—near the water! If you're out in a boat, scan the offshore islands for rookeries.

May 18, 1995

HARMLESS GOLD

*"Dear common flower, that grow'st beside the way,
Fringing the dusty road with harmless gold...
My childhood's earliest thoughts are linked with thee..."*

Lawns and grassy areas are already studded with the "harmless gold" to which James Russell Lowell refers in his poem, "To a Dandelion". The common dandelion, listed as an "alien" in flower guides, was not part of the North American flora when the first settlers arrived from Europe. Its introduction was intentional, not accidental. It came to New England in the 17th-century with English immigrants, and during the 18th-century folks emigrating from Germany to establish farms in eastern Pennsylvania included dandelion seeds in their sea-chests.

To put it mildly, the plant has thrived. It is now found from shore to shore, just about everywhere the sun shines! It is loved; it is deplored. Its young leaves are relished as salad; its flowers are distilled into wine; its roots are steeped into medicines. It is mowed down with a vengeance by lawn-lovers—but still, in the summer and fall there are myriads of seed-globes, each seed equipped with silky sails, for merry children to blow into the wind. Some of the seeds will start new dandelion plants; others will be eaten by goldfinches or chipping sparrows.

Contrary to the "general rule" that composites are late-season bloomers, dandelion blooms as soon as do our native woodland wildflowers—trout lily, bloodroot, etc.—and it will continue to blossom even into October. Furthermore, the plant is a perennial and has a long, fleshy taproot. It will not be banished!

Extremely rich in vitamins and minerals, it has been determined that field-grown dandelion contains half again as much Vitamin A as spinach and more than ten times as much as lettuce. No wonder it was early recognized as an effective "spring tonic". Our early settlers knew nothing about vitamins but after a long winter during which the only vegetables eaten were those which had been canned from last year's garden, the early green leaves and buds satisfied a craving—a need.

In the Pennsylvania countryside it is common, even now, to see on cold March or early April days, folks stooping in the fields, a basket or paper bag alongside each. They're after a "mess of dandelion." It's a real spring treat in that part of the country. The salad of early greens (the younger the more delicious, and the embryo flower buds best of all) served with hot bacon dressing and hard-boiled egg is unique to the Pennsylvania Dutch area. When I mentioned once to a Maine friend that we preferred dandelion raw in salad, she promptly replied, "Oh no! We boil them."

In each flower-head there are about 100 tiny florets, each a perfect, self-pollinating flower! Each head is borne upon a long, slender, leafless, hollow, milky stem. Did you ever, as a child, pluck the flower, split the base of its stem, and then push with your tongue until you had two corkscrew curls? I did, and today the taste of the dandelion recalls childhood playmates on sunny lawns, happily making curls!

"Who would banish it from the meadows or lawns, where it copies in gold upon the green expanse, the stars of the midnight sky?" — John Burroughs

May 12, 1994

DANDELION DRESSING

4 slices of bacon
1/2 cup of cream
2 tablespoons vinegar
2 eggs

2 tablespoons sugar
2 tablespoons bacon fat
Pinch of salt

Fry the bacon slowly until crisp. Remove bacon and fat from pan. Measure fat, return to pan, add cream, and blend over slow heat. Beat eggs together, add salt, sugar and vinegar, and mix with slightly warmed cream. Pour into double boiler, and stir until it becomes a custard. Pour warm over dandelion greens. (Also great on endive!). Garnish with crumbled bacon pieces.

SPRING PEEPERS

We first heard the spring peepers, this year, on Apr. 9, 1980. It was a relatively weak chorus compared to the volume these tiny creatures will attain as spring progresses. To hear that treble chorus lifts one's heart. We pass along the happy word, "We heard the peepers last night", just as we ask, "Did you hear the wild geese this morning?" It gives one a sort of "All's right with the world!" feeling.

Although they are noisy and numerous, these little amphibians are seldom seen by humans. The full grown adult tree frog is no more than one and one-half inches long. Brownish or grayish, it bears on its back a dark St. Andrew's cross which explains its species name *crucifer*. *Hyla crucifer* is his impressive scientific name, *hyla* being the Greek word for forest.

Peepers are part of the teeming life of small freshwater ponds, bogs, and marshes. This treefrog spends most of the year in damp woodlands or meadows, feeding principally upon insects during the warm months and hibernating beneath the surface of the ground during winter. Then, when the mean temperature—the isotherm—has reached 50°F., *hyla crucifer* is ready to start the new year. Marvelously, "Your peeper makes a calculation which would baffle a meteorologist," writes Dr. Joseph Wood Krutch in *The Twelve Seasons*. "He takes into consideration the maximum to which the temperature has risen, the minimum to which it has fallen during the night, the relative length of the warmer and the colder periods, besides, no doubt, other factors hard to get down in tables or charts. But at last he knows that the moment has come."

The male peeper returns to his pond or goes to another, clambers up a cattail stalk, alder stem, or pussy willow twig, and inflates his throat pouch. He appears to be gripping a balloon with his chin, and with this bubble trills his mating call which can be heard half a mile away. He is not alone, of course. There are scores of peepers, all peeping. The females (they have no pouch) respond by coming to the pond or pool where on underwater plants deep enough to avoid a late freeze, they deposit their eggs, spaced singly, fertilized as they are laid. A protective jelly-like substance covers the eggs which will hatch in a matter of days, perhaps from seven to ten, depending upon the temperature.

This next stage is the tadpole phase of the frog's life history. He's in danger, immediately—as, indeed, he was when in the egg. He's considered a delicacy by small fish, insects, adult frogs, mammals such as mink and raccoon. A snapping turtle poses a terrible threat to young *hyla crucifers*!

Then too, the tadpoles and eggs are vulnerable to the curiosity and acquisitiveness of young boys and girls. Eggs one week, tadpoles the next, are carried home in jars or buckets of pond water. It can be a fascinating experience to observe, in an aquarium, the transformation of these amphibians. If the project is to be successful, from both the frog's and child's point of view, pond water must be used, a few water

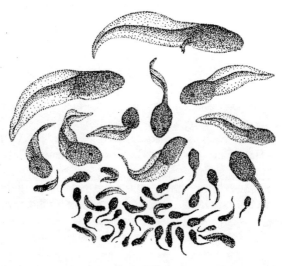

plants should be added, and the container should be placed where it will receive sun for part of the day. As they hatch, only a few tadpoles should be kept. The rest should be returned to the pond and the unhatched eggs must be discarded.

The young tadpoles will nibble at green pond scum or at partially decaying spinach or lettuce, and at algae which form on the growing plants and aquarium sides. The tail, slowly being absorbed, actually provides most of the nourishment needed at this stage. As the tail becomes shorter, the appearance and growth of legs is fun to watch. A board or other device should be provided so that the frog or near-frog can climb out of the water and into the air. By this time his gills have been covered up and his lungs have developed. He must breathe air, although he can remain under water for long periods of time.

When the metamorphosis is complete there is a big-eyed, tail-less frog. He has a backbone strong enough to support him on land, four limbs, a heart, lungs, and a highly developed digestive system. He has teeth and a tongue which equip him for eating meat. He can live on land.

Yet, as a baby he resembled a fish—and a poor fish at that! He was able to do no more than scrape at soft vegetable material. He represents tremendous progress, a real success in evolution. It was something like 340 million years ago that the first pioneer fish began the long process which resulted in enabling vertebrate animals to live on land. The fish evolved into what we call amphibians. The Greek word *amphibios* means leading a double life. Amphibians spend part of their life history (egg and larval stages) in water and part of it (adult) on land. Some 50 million years later reptiles, able to lay their eggs on land, developed.

If you're working with children and want to go in for raising frogs or salamanders from eggs, or offering temporary homes to turtles or other pond creations, I urge you to secure *Pets From The Pond* by Margaret Waring Buck. Also excellent is the *Golden Nature Guide*, "Pond Life".

With a sense of wonder let us keep our ears attuned
these spring evenings for the peepers' chorus.
"Long since have I marveled
How of ten thousand creatures there is not one
But has its tune."

Ou-Yang Hsis (A.D. 1007-72)

April 24, 1980

BARBERRY BARBS

In an open space a bit downslope from our deck grows a shrub which only birds would have planted. It was here in 1971 when we bought these two acres, a small part of what had once been a farm. Now, as a result of nature's efforts to reclaim the land as forest, there are white and yellow birch trees, red oaks, red and white spruces, and white pine tall enough to have given this area its present name, "Tallwood." Already well estimated in 1971 there were also wild shrubs—winterberry (a deciduous holly, sometimes referred to as black alder), beaked hazelnut, and Japanese barberry.

Japanese barberry, as its specific name suggests, is not a Native American shrub but was introduced as an ornamental, commonly used as a hedge. It's a very effective hedge, too, as I learned early in my life. When I was ten years old my family moved from a very flat community to Nutley, N.J. which was in the foothills of the Watchung Mountains. Our new house was at the crest of a hill which afforded wonderful sledding in winter. But this was late August and it occurred to me that it would be wonderful to roll down the sidewalk on skates. It was a beautiful morning, everything fresh with dew sparkling in early sunlight. I buckled on my skates and started to coast downhill—soon realizing I could not cope with anything so steep. Rather than wait for an inevitable crash, I veered onto the narrow margin of grass between the concrete sidewalk and—a barberry hedge, into which I plunged. I can still feel the burning sensation of those stinging thorns and also the cool splashes of dew on my skin. I was chagrined. I don't believe I even mentioned the incident at breakfast—but I was older and wiser. I knew that barberry shrubs have masses of sharp spikes and I knew that Daily Street was too steep for roller-skating!

The barberry shrub on our property is easily identified as the Japanese variety by the arrangement of its berries.

They are borne singly along the stem whereas the berries of common barberry dangle in racemes like loose clusters of grapes. Common barberry was introduced from Europe by early settlers, although its origin had been mountainous areas of Asia. Only one barberry is native to our eastern states. That is American barberry and its range is limited to wooded mountain areas of Virginia and Georgia.

The genus is well-named. Each species has "barbs" (although not the fishhook type) and small berries which range in color from red to blue. All of our three eastern species bear red berries.

Some of last year's crop of berries still cling to our shrub in this first week of May, but most of them have already been eaten by birds and perhaps mice. In mid-April when we noticed movement in the barberry, we soon realized that a robin had found and was consuming the berries. Although tasteless now, they are still soft and springy whereas the berries of the nearby winterberry are dry and crisp.

In *The Natural History of Wild Shrubs and Vines,* Donald Stokes urges us to pay special attention to barberry in the springtime. It's fresh green leaves, when chewed, "have a pleasant, acidic flavor, very similar to that of sheep-sorrel leaves". Nibble them for a taste of spicy juice or toss them into a mixed salad for added tang.

Another reason Donald Stokes wants us not to miss noticing barberry in springtime is because of its interesting yellow flowers which hang below the branches. Not especially pretty, their odor is almost unpleasant. They usually are unnoticed by humans but the bees know when the nectar is ready. If you're lucky enough to observe the pollination act, you'll witness a fascinating procedure. Several stamens (male) surround the post-like pistil (female part) in the center of the flower. At the base of the stamens is the treasured nectar. As the bee's mouth enters the nectaries, the action causes the stamens to spring inward so that when the bee emerges the sides of its face are brushed with pollen. "Each stamen can spring independently so that the bee may be snapped upon as many as six times." Stokes suggests that we simulate this process and activate the floral mechanism, by gently applying a fine pine needle to the base of the stamens. Look for pollen on your pine needle as you remove it. "The flowere is a marvelous little event, and once you experience it I guarantee you will come back to visit the plant each spring."

The berries develop during the summer, green at first, gradually becoming the characteristic bright scarlet. They are edible and tastiest just after becoming red. Try them raw; they also make a pleasant jam. In fact, one of the reasons that common barberry was first brought to America by settlers is that its fruits were used for jellies. Another reason is that the plant's bright yellow sap has been used for dyeing wool and other cloth. This species was soon in disfavor because it was discovered to be a host for a wheat fungus. Efforts—ineffectual—were made to eradicate it. Japanese barberry is, strangely, immune to the fungus.

Barberry is here to stay, principally because its berries are eaten by birds. The pulp is digested; the seeds are defecated still intact and coated with fertilizer! Perhaps the berries are tasteless by wintertime but they must surely be nutritious and certainly welcome when there is little else to choose from. Ruffed grouse, bobwhite, pheasant, mockingbird, and cedar waxwing are among the birds who consume these berries—and we know that robins will in a pinch! Surely, too, the thick tangle of twigs must provide good nesting sites to many species.

Now—locate the barberry shrub near you, nibble some of its fresh green tangy leaves, and try to observe that pollination act!

May 8, 1986

THE RED-EYED VIREO

Among Maine's small, summer songbirds are the red-eyed vireos. Many of us who like to walk in the woods and who are alert to what goes on in the natural world have never seen, knowingly, a red-eyed vireo. Yet, this little worm-eating songbird is one of the most abundant in the eastern woodlands. It prefers a stand of deciduous trees, but it also inhabits mixed evergreen-deciduous woods as well as parks, farm areas, orchards, etc. This species begins to arrive in Maine about the first of May, and is a common sight from mid-May through August. Vireos may linger in our area into October although most of them leave for the southland (our southern states and Central America) in early September.

Although we may not see it, if a pair is nearby we will hear the male's song. Over and over again, all day long and every day he announces, "Vireo, vireo, I am green, I am green..." ("I am green" is the literal translation of the Latin verb *vireo*). The male repeats his phrase, sometimes alternately with the inflection of a question and then of a statement. Indeed, he is green and a soft, inconspicuous, olive-green at that. The scientific name for the species is *vireo olivaceus*. If you could come up close to one as I once had the opportunity, you'd see that the eye really is ruby-red. There's a prominent white eyebrow stripe accented with black bordering lines. The crown is gray, the breast is white, and there are no wing-bars. There are no visible differences between the sexes. Behavior is our only clue. The most obvious is that the male does all the singing. If we do locate a nest, we can know that the bird which is incubating is the female.

Availability of food is what dictates when a bird should arrive on its nesting territory. Most of the vireos and warblers depend principally upon leaf-eating insects and therefore they comprise the bulk of the second wave of migrants. When the canopy of green leaves is spreading and becoming deeper in tone, these tiny birds arrive to enliven our woodlands and to keep the leafeaters in check. Warbler-sized, vireos are less flitting than warblers. Their search for crawling food on the undersides of leaves is slow, methodical, and successful!

Within a short time, nesting territories will be selected and declared by the males, and partnerships settled upon. Then each pair, with approximately two claimed acres, will proceed with the important business of raising a family. However, it is the female who chooses the nestsite and she alone will incubate the three to five white eggs, sparsely speckled with ruddy brown. The male will sing to her throughout the twelve to fourteen days she is brooding the eggs and he will, so it seems, suggest to her when she should leave the nest for a meal. She joins him. Sometimes he feeds her and sometimes just stays nearby while she feeds herself.

When the eggs have hatched, the father bird's role is different. He does feed the chicks, sometimes directly, and sometimes he delivers food to his mate which she then distributes to the babies. During the first few days of the hatching phase, the mother broods them but by the sixth day they will be feathered enough—and hungry enough—that both parents will be kept busy satisfying the growing nestlings.

One memorable spring when our children were youngsters, we discovered a red-eyed vireo nest during the incubation period. Although the cup-shaped, pensile cradle was about ten feet above the foot of the ironwood tree in which it was placed, the tree grew from the base of a seven-foot bank and our path led along the top of the bank. So here was a red-eyed vireo nest on the children's eye level! The mother soon grew to trust us. We'd watch, one or two of us at a time and observe the mother reach out for the dangling span worms which were exceptionally abundant that year. "She's hungry!" reasoned the children, "but she can't leave her nest." So they helped. Before long the brooding bird confidently accepted the green, crawling worms from their fingers!

That was in 1953. The oldest of our four children, Mary Liz, was eleven years old. Recently she came upon the notes she made that spring. They follow:

"May 24. Nest discovered in afternoon. One vireo egg, one cowbird egg. Female was sitting on nest in evening. Laying egg?

May 25, 8:30 a.m. Two vireo eggs, one cowbird egg.

May 26. Early morning. Raining. Adult on nest.

May 27. Three vireo eggs, bird incubating. Removed cowbird egg with spoon.

May 28. I touched her beak. She stayed on nest. Brave or afraid?

May 29. Fed her worms while on nest.

May 30. A very rainy day.

May 31. Took worm from me but did not eat.

June 1. Flew away when I came near. *(Did she prefer to join her mate?—F.L.H.)*

June 2. Flew away again.

June 8. Two eggs hatched today, one is still an egg.

June 9. The two birds seem very weak. Mother seems afraid. Other egg has not hatched.

June 10. Birds have grown bigger and stronger.

June 11. Babies much bigger and stronger.

June 17. Eyes are open; they made their first peep today.

June 21. One bird has gone.

June 22. Rain—both gone."

Then we could examine the nest and found it to be quite typical. It was secured to the fork of the tree by gossamer spider web that finest yet strongest of all threads. These will hold through the fiercest summer storms. The fibers which composed the body of the nest were strips of birch and grape bard, rootlets, grasses, and then finer grasses for the lining. Cocoons, bits of wasp or spider nests, lichens, leaves and mosses, are often used as ornaments. Sometimes a false bottom is constructed to avoid incubating that almost inevitable cowbird egg!

May 19, 1988

WOODLAND ELVES

If you read Barnaby Porter's *A Midnight Raid* in the Feb. 22, 1989 issue of *Coastal Journal* you know that Barnaby has not only identified the nocturnal creatures that have so drastically diminished his supply of sunflower seeds meant for birds but has actually "caught them in the act."

The raiders were flying squirrels. Elf-like, nocturnal in habits, seldom leaving any discernible tracks or other evidence of its presence, this little squirrel is actually common throughout New England's wooded areas. Yet very few people ever see one.

There are two species, both of which inhabit mature woodlands of mixed deciduous/evergreen trees. It is likely that in our area the northern flying squirrel, *glaucomys sabrinus*, is the sprite which Barnaby Porter observed. It is slightly larger than its cousin, *glaucomys volans*. Both species are pretty animals with large luminous dark eyes and pelts of thick soft fur. Both have dark backs and light bellies with the northern squirrel having the darker back and the southern one having the whiter belly.

Of course, they don't actually fly. They glide. They vol-plane. If you could see a flying squirrel at rest you'd think its skin was too big for its body. It seems to be gathered into folds between its front and hind legs. But when the little fellow is ready to glide into the evening, he stretches out all four limbs and that loose membrane becomes taut, creating a planing surface somewhat like that of a kite. He can steer a course by maneuvering his legs and he can brake by dropping his furred tail, which he then jerks up just before landing. The glide is usually commenced from a high branch and its general direction is, of course, downward.

In *The Quadrupeds of North America* (c. 1850), John James Audubon and The Rev. John Bachman relate how, in a Pennsylvania meadow "containing here and there immense oak and beech trees", they witnessed a remarkable exhibition of these nocturnal rodents in action. As dusk approached "one emerged from its hole and ran up to the top of a tree; another soon followed, and ere long dozens came forth, and commenced their graceful flights from some upper branch to a lower bough..." The glides were repeated many times. "Crowds of these little creatures joined in these sportive gambols; there could not have been less than two hundred. Scores of them would leave each tree at the same moment, and cross each other, gliding like spirits through the air, seeming to have no other object in view than to indulge a playful propensity. We watched and mused till the last shadows of day had disappeared."

Like chickadees and woodpeckers, flying squirrels are cavity nesters. And like red and gray squirrels, they are resourceful. A natural cavity in a dead tree is just fine—but a previously used woodpecker excavated hole will do just as well. A house set out for bird tenants will serve beautifully and if the entrance hole is too small, the flying squirrel has no trouble enlarging it. One late afternoon in June we watched three young flying squirrels and no adult crawl out of a birdbox which the year before had housed chickadees. It may have been their first trip into the big world outside—their mother was quite solicitous. If the natural food situation appears good, but all the dead trees in an area have been removed and no birdhouses are available, flying squirrels may move into an attic where accommodations are likely to be quite comfortable.

Tom Fegely, a writer for *The Morning Call*, Allentown, Pa., relates how, when he was working with junior high school students as their outdoor education director, a whole class became involved in a fascinating experience. One of the boys had "live-trapped eight adult flying squirrels from his grandmother's attic" and brought them to school. Seven of these were released in more suitable locations. But they kept the plump female who, two days before Easter, gave birth to three pink, blind, naked babies. The mother had become accustomed to the children and allowed them to feed her and to handle her and her offspring. Dry dog food, seeds and fruit kept her healthy. One morning, however, they found her, drowned, in a 50-gallon aquarium. Somehow she had escaped from her cage, glided about the schoolroom, landed in the water and, could not escape from the glass container. The children fed and cared for her young orphans until early June. By then the squirrels had developed luxuriant dark brown fur coats and were able to eat seeds and nuts on their own. The students released their charges in suitable habitats. By providing the young squirrels with peanut butter on crackers, Tom was able to keep them still long enough to photograph them. That picture was printed in a *Ranger Rick* magazine in the early 1970s. What a wonderful project for those boys and girls!

There was a happy summer when our children, ranging in age then from five to thirteen years, fed flying squirrels. We had had some peanuts, meant for birds, on the railing of an upstairs landing. One of the children spied a big-eyed, pretty mammal nibbling a peanut. "Mommy! Daddy! What animal is this? It's not a chipmunk and besides, it's already dark outside!" We checked our field guide and determined that it was a flying squirrel. We were surprised that it showed no fear although we stood on the other side of a glass door only two feet away. It wasn't long (a few evenings) before the flying squirrel would accept a peanut from the children's hands or stay and nibble a hand-held, peanut butter-spread cracker. Although the squirrel's toenails were not retracted, as a friendly cat's might be, they never scratched—"just tickled". We all grew fond of the trusting little fellows, invited other children to see the show, and generally enjoyed the relationship. But then, some nights, we heard the distinctive hissing sound of a barn owl and in a very short time no flying squirrel came to us for a treat. A barn owl is described as "gliding swiftly, unerringly, and noiselessly upon its pray." It is extremely beneficial in rodent control—but we were prejudiced. We missed our evening visitors—the friendly sprites of the woodland.

Northern flying squirrels, like human children seem to actually enjoy the snow. They tunnel in it and will be active on it when the temperature is at 10°F. They do have predators—weasels, great-horned owls, fishers, and house cats. In the warm seasons, tree-climbing snakes enjoy a meal of flying squirrel.

Although I hope that the flying squirrels which Barnaby Porter observed are not nesting in his attic, I also hope that he and his family enjoy their flying squirrels even to the point of feeding them peanut-butter treats from their hands.

Mar. 2, 1989

NATURE'S SCAVENGERS

Along with happy sightings of returning songbirds—tree swallows, phoebes, flickers, and bluebirds—there have been several reports of turkey vultures (*cathartes aura*) being seen.

The presence of turkey vultures in Maine was real news just a few decades ago. The birds are still uncommon here but each year more of them are seen and the species is now known to breed in our state.

This bird is a true scavenger. Its food is carrion—the flesh of an already dead animal. It has been said of a vulture that "unlike his raptor cousins, he does not bring death, he only attends it." Therefore he is not feared by other creations; yet... "when the buzzard lost his ability of kill and embraced a post-mortem cuisine, he became the most despised of birds," (John Madson). Somehow the vultures evolved without sharp, powerful talons but did develop amazingly sharp, farseeing eyes. Its beak is a marvelous tool for tearing flesh; the featherless head can be plunged deep into a carcass; it can soar tirelessly while searching for—a dead creature. It is superbly adapted to its way of life, although it seems repulsive to us.

And the vulture does fill a needed niche. A southern farmer seldom needs to bury a dead animal. He can leave it where it falls—or drag it into a corner and let the vultures clean it up. Why have they moved into Maine? Do we have more road-killed animals? And, when we walk in the woods, do we see a dead creature? The natural scavengers, some of them insects, some of them mammals, have recycled them into food.

Neither the turkey vulture nor the black vulture, its cousin with a more southerly range, do anything about constructing a nest. They may clear the selected site (usually a natural shelter, such as a ledge), where the eggs, probably two, are deposited. The turkey vulture nests earlier in the south but in Maine the breeding cycle begins in late April. Both parents incubate the eggs over quite a long period—38 to 41 days, almost six weeks.

The babies will be covered with long, white down; the head will be bare and black, with a meager bit of white down on the crown. Both adults will feed the homely chicks by regurgitation. The youngsters are active from the beginning. They will not be fully feathered until the tenth week after hatching and they'll fly at eleven weeks. The heads will remain black, perhaps for most of their first year. It's the red head of the adult which is responsible for the common name. Does it suggest a turkey's wattles?

Perhaps the naked head is partly responsible for the fact that although in warmer climates vultures are permanent residents, those that have moved into New England migrate to spend the winter in our warmer states.

The turkey vulture has been scornfully called "the gloomiest bird", the "skunk of the bird world" and demeaned for what is probably its only defense tactic. When assailed, it vomits on the aggressor; the resulting odor is very foul—but the method is effective!

Now, having heard of the vulture's unpleasant, actually repugnant features, let's hear something nice about it. John Madson phrases it this way: "...he is among the most beautiful birds on the wing. Few other American birds possess such majesty of flight. He leaves all ugliness on the earth below, and after the first wing strokes as he labors heavily away from his carrion—and as he earns enough altitude to find the thermal updrafts and the high, tending winds—he becomes a floating mote of infinite grace."

I, personally, associate "the buzzard" as we called it in New Jersey, with a very happy day. It was in 1930 and I was a counselor in the Montclair, N.J. Girl Scout camp in Stokes State Forest. A hike to Sunrise Mountain was planned. About ten of us left base camp at 3 a.m. and drove to where we could take the trail. Then, with breakfast gear and food on our backs we hiked to the peak, having stopped at "Spring Cabin" to fill our canteens and to have a drink of wonderful water. We arrived in time for a very beautiful sunrise, then cooked our breakfast and ate it. Then, replete but weary, we stretched out on the mountaintop and relaxed in the warm sun.

When I opened my eyes, I saw only tall grasses gleaming in the sunshine, the green of a few shrubs, a deep blue sky, and—big black birds, three I think, soaring so effortlessly. As I watched they circled over where we lay and seemed to come nearer—lower. Was I the only one awake? I knew they were buzzards and we must have been raising their hopes for a meal. I waved an arm and called. A couple of girls sat up—and the buzzards flew away in disappointment.

If you own, or can borrow, *A Treasury of Birdlore* edited by Joseph Wood Krutch and Paul S. Eriksson, read *An Adventure with a Turkey Vulture* by George Miksch Sutton. It is truly an amazing story!

April 21, 1994

THE LOVELIEST OF TREES

"Loveliest of trees, the cherry now
Is hung with snow along the bough

And since to look at things in bloom
Fifty springs are little room,
About the woodlands I will go
To see the cherry hung with snow."

These are the first two and the last four lines of Alfred Edward Housman's poem which is probably familiar to more people than is any other poetic reference to the cherry tree. A.E. (as many of his poems were signed) wrote *Loveliest of Trees* in 1879. It is easy to empathize with the youth who outlived "threescore years and ten", thus having seven extra springs in which to "look at things in bloom."

In Lincoln County we have three native cherry trees, these are: pin (or fire) cherry, choke cherry, and black cherry. Of these, fire cherry is the first to flower. Its white blossoms are held in short, umbrella-like clusters. This shrubby species often springs up after an area has been clear-cut or burned over. Choke cherry blooms just after the shadblow does and the black cherry's blossoms usually open while the choke cherry is still blooming. The flowers of these two are borne on long clusters called *recemes*. If you'd like to differentiate between the leaves of the cherries, I recommend *A Field Guide to Trees and Shrubs* by Petrides (Houghton Mifflin).

Maine also has cherries which have escaped into the wild, having been planted by settlers in colonial days, and some special varieties have been planted on private properties.

In *New England's Prospect* which was published in London in 1639, William Wood referred briefly in a poem to the wild cherry as "Within this Indian orchard fruits be some—the ruddy cherry..." In prose, however, he was quite articulate and not very complimentary to our native cherries. "The cherry

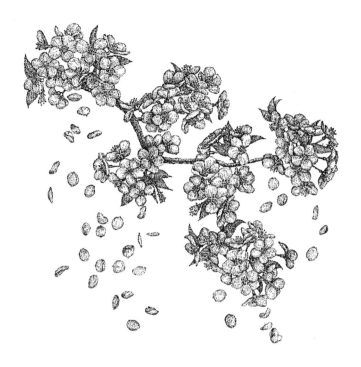

trees yield great store of cherries, which grow on clusters like grapes; they be much smaller than our English cherry, nothing near so good if they be not ripe. They so furr the mouth that the tongue will cling to the roof, and the throat wax hoarse with swallowing those red bullies...English ordering may bring them to an English cherry, but they are as wild as the Indians."

It is entirely true that the fruit of neither the choke cherry nor the black cherry tree is sweet. The black variety is termed "edible but slightly bitter," and the choke cherry "highly astringent". William Wood must have tried the choke cherry. We would say that it "puckers the mouth" but "furr" is more vividly descriptive.

The English never did pick up the challenge to "order" the choke cherry. Most of the colonies were readily hospitable to

English cherries. Settlers had the "pies" (*prunus cerasus*) and the "sweets" (*prunus avium*) under cultivation in the 17th-century. But in Quebec, where the climate is too rugged for the pie or sweet cherry to thrive..."the habitants have long cultivated the choke cherry and have selected strains that may be eaten out of hand, like the best orchard cherries..." (Donald Culross Peattie). As we find them wild in Maine today they make a really good jelly (with pectin or apple added) and they are sought for wine. American Indians make a paste from choke cherries which they used to flavor pemmican.

Of all the cherries, the wood of only the black cherry is of commercial value. The tree attains a good size (up to 5' diameter and 60'-80' tall is typical). Cherry furniture is prized for its hardness, its close grain, and its warm color. It makes a perfectly beautiful floor.

Cherry trees are of great value to wildlife. "Hoofed browsers and rabbits feed extensively on the twigs, foliage, and bark of wild cherries" (quoted from *American Wildlife and Plants—A Guide to Wildlife Food Habits* by Martin, Zim, and Nelson [Dover]). Also the bark is sometimes used for flavoring. Nevertheless, the leaves, twigs, and seeds contain hydrocyanic acid. Under some conditions ingestion of these has sickened and sometimes killed browsing cattle and horses For humans and domestic animals all of the cherry tree should be considered potentially dangerous—except the fruit.

Clearly, the leaves are not toxic to the many insects whose larvae feed upon them. These are a favorite food of the *cecropia* and *promethea* caterpillars, both of which are classed as "giant silk moths". One year we "raised" *cecropia* moths from eggs and tiny caterpillars which a friend had given us. Some of the larvae we kept inside, providing them with twigs of fresh cherry leaves each day until they were large and ready to spin their cocoons. Our grandson, Jeff, was a little boy then; he participated in the project and brought a few of the cocoons home to Bethlehem, Pa. The next spring, he and some of his kindergarten friends watched the emergence of the big, beautiful moths. The rest of the worms we put on a wild cherry tree on our property. Of these, almost all were eaten by birds. Nestlings of warblers and many other songbirds are fed these crawlers by the beakfull.

Another less pleasant caterpillar likes to feed upon cherry leaves. That's the tent caterpillar. Its webby night-shelters mar the beauty of so many wild cherry trees. But here's another example of interdependency in nature. One of our best chances to see a cuckoo is in a cherry tree. The cuckoo is not after the cherries. It is there to feast upon the prickly caterpillar which few other birds will eat.

The fruits of all cherry trees are relished by many species of songbirds and by grouse, quail, and pheasant. Among the mammals which enjoy cherries are raccoon, black bear, red fox, deer, cottontail rabbit, and gray squirrel. When the cherries are ripe it is a lovely sight to see a flock of cedar waxwings feasting on the fruits. This pretty bird is often nicknamed "cherry bird".

So do notice and enjoy our wild cherry trees—now, while they are in blossom, and later when they are red with cherries.

June 2, 1988

THE LONELY LOON

To spend the third week of May at Kidney Pond Camps in Baxter Park has become a happy habit with us. And, although it means returning to a familiar place in the same part of the year, each time we go that week has its own features and is memorable in its own way.

We always canoe on some of the several small lakes clustered in the southwestern sector of the park. This year we paddled on Kidney Pond, of course, and on Lily Pad and Jackson Ponds. And we always walk the trails to other ponds (Rocky, Draper, Celia, and Deer Ponds, this year), either from our home lake or from another spot. One day this May, we hiked to Windy Pitch Pond from the trail linking Lily Pad Pond and "Niagara Falls". Each year we hear and see loons and we've always seen moose; yet we have different experiences with those wild denizens of the northern woods every time we're there.

We always are delighted with the wildflowers and ferns and mosses along the trails, and with the northern shrubs

which grow at the water's edge. This year the flowers were further advanced than in usual, for Piscataquis County had its unseasonably early heat-wave, too. Trailing arbutus was at its peak when we arrived on the 18th; the petals were falling by the time we left on the 25th. Painted trillium was in full bloom, brightening the trail-sides all week; star flower and goldthread sparkled amid the moss and leaf-litter; the rhodora was gorgeous, glowing at the edges of all the ponds. Pink (and white) moccasin flowers were just popping through their protective sheaths and wild lily-of-the-valley was still in bud, as was ours when we arrived home.

The mosses were lush and green: fern fronds were almost fully expanded. I identified "leather leaf", a shrub new to me. It grows profusely in shallow water, its white, bell-like flowers closely resembling those of blueberries. But its leaves, leathery and evergreen, and its many-seeded fruits, not at all tempting to humans, are used by wildlife only as subsistence fare in harsh times.

The weather was better in the mountains that week than you had along the coast. There were two absolutely perfect days when mile-high Mt. Katahdin, still with streaks of snow on its upper slopes, loomed high and clear to the east of Kidney Pond and when the lesser peaks—OJI, Doubletop, Mt. Coe or North Brother, South Brother, Barren Mountain or Squaw's Bosom were plainly visible from one lake or another. The Sentinel (a mere 1750 feet high but a challenging climb for most of us) is wooded to its top. It's the peak closest to Kidney Pond; the sun sets behind it. Even on the days that were gray, we had glimpses of the peaks, sometimes wreathed in mist. The rain, when it came, was intermittent. It freshened the mosses and ferns, made everything fragrant and—gave us a good excuse to stick around camp and absorb the beauty so close at hand.

The moose walked around camp, swam and/or waded across the lake and along its shores, actually approaching, rather than retreating from, the folks who sought their pictures. Chris and Pat Bauer and Francis and Mary Calvert were with us. They are all active members of the Lincoln County Camera Club; there should be a good photographic record of the week's fun and beauty. One morning (one of the partly rainy days) we walked the easy trail to Deer Pond and found it rimmed with rhodora in full bloom. There was no wind; the rosy border was mirrored in the water as were the mountains in the background. Mrs. Calvert worked with her camera to compose her picture and just as she was satisfied—into her frame walked a big bull moose. "Oh, it was just perfect!"

We saw a deer, several snowshoe rabbits, and a weasel. He was a beautiful little mammal and came quite close to us from under a turned-over canoe at Celia Pond. His coat, in full summer brown now, will turn to white next winter and then he'll be known as an ermine.

As always, the calls of the loons are what emphasize the wildness of the area. Loons, because they are so awkward and so handicapped on land, must nest at the edge of still water. The wakes of the motorboats have driven loons away from many of our lakes. But in Baxter Park no motors are permitted; the loons are at home on the ponds.

We were puzzled to realize that three loons considered Kidney Pond their own home territory and we were also puzzled by their calls. In the middle of the night, we'd be wakened to hear a shrill, ardent phrase—then an answer—then a mingling of the two voices, a duet which sometimes was actually musical. Then, again, we'd hear a monotonous, question-like call, repeated in a minor key. And it was never answered. In the daytime two loons, obviously paired, swam more or less together, sometimes even touching bills. Their devotion was evident. The other loon was always alone. Charlie Norris, the camp proprietor, told me the story:

"That loon haunts me. I'm sure it's a female and the widow of a loon which died at this end of the lake three or four years ago. It was before camp opened and the ice-out was late that year. Here at the head of the lake, dammed in among cakes of ice, was a dead loon. I managed to reach it and lift it out of the water. Then I realized that out beyond the ice cakes was another loon—very agitated. I was walking away with her mate. I'm positive. Every year since then she's back and she gives that same mournful call. It's like, "Where are you? Where are you?"

Loons mate for life. The fact that the lone loon is accepted on this small pond by the other two, supports the thought that the loner is a female. A male would most likely be considered by the paired male a rival for his mate and a contestant for his territory. As it is, the three share the same water amicably.

It's a poignant, little story—we could call it, "The Legend of the Lonely Loon."

Do you wonder that this place is like a magnet to us?

May 31, 1979

Editor's Note: The mountain, OJI, was so named because the glaciers that scraped it left markings which seem to make the letters OJI.
—MLHB

SUMMER

Life has loveliness to sell,
All beautiful and splendid things,
Blue waves whitened on a cliff,
Soaring fire that sways and sings,
And children's faces looking up,
Holding wonder like a cup.

—Sara Teasdale

CANOEING

We've enjoyed canoeing on Maine ponds since the third week of May in 1974 when we first stayed at Kidney Pond Camps in Baxter Park. That week sharpened our desire to have our own canoe.

Soon after returning to Boothbay we purchased a 13-ft fiberglass Lincoln. It was the right choice for us. It's light enough in weight and short enough in length that two of us can easily mount it onto the rack of our VW. Our son, Tony, lifts it alone with ease. The material is readily repaired if damaged (but we find it impervious to normal bumps) and it's quiet in use.

Wood-and-canvas canoes are quiet also—but more expensive and heavier. Aluminum canoes resound every slap of water, frightening wildlife. Our canoe has a keel. We find it a responsive vehicle, yet stable, easy to keep on course.

Since we've owned our little yellow canoe we've explored Adam's, West Harbor, Sherman's, and Kimbletown ponds. On a very calm day we've paddled on Linekin Bay as far to the west as Lobster Cove and we spent much of one day on Great Salt Bay, launching at Lewis Point. We were unprepared, though, for how the changing tide would influence our progress.

We've decided to be pond paddlers, leaving tidal and white river water to the experts. This summer we have canoed on a cove of Damariscotta Lake (exciting, with nesting bald eagles and loons within sound of Route 215's traffic) and Biscay Pond lures us.

But I doubt that any body of water will enchant us more than does West Harbor Pond in Boothbay Harbor. It's really beautiful and can only be fully appreciated from a canoe. You can admire the lovely, unspoiled, and often rugged shoreline from the middle of the pond, and you can paddle up close to the edges of mainland and islands for detail.

Here's a brief recount of some of the most interesting things we've observed during our many times of paddling the perimeter of West Harbor Pond.

Wildflowers: The lovely fragrant water-lily, *nymphaea odorata*, gleams bright and white where the water is shallow, its roots in mud, its stems in water, its pad-like leaves floating on the surface, its blossoms and buds held just above the water. These open in early morning and close soon after noon, each individual flower expanded for only three or four days. In some places there are pink water-lilies; these may be the roseate form of the same species or they may be a rose-colored water-lily which was introduced from Europe, planted here and become naturalized.

Other coves are yellow with spatterdock, *numphar advena*, also called yellow pond lily, cow lily, and bull lily. Having watched moose at Baxter Park wade into the water, bend and forage for the roots of this plant, we know the reason for two of its common names. The moose, emerging with horns draped with greenery and dripping with water is a comical sight!

The shallow edges of the pond are blue with pickerelweed in August. Arrowhead, (white, 3-petaled flowers and arrow shaped leaves) grows among the pickerelweed, which also has an arrow shaped leaf but with blunt lobes.

Another plant which is abundant along the shore of West Harbor Pond is cattail. Both species, common and narrow-leaved, are present. The latter is distinguished from the common by a space between the masses of pistillate and staminate flowers, whereas on the common cattail the male and female flowers are contiguous. The pistillate flowers on both varieties darken as they mature. The stalks, tipped with brown velvet tails, are popular for winter bouquets. Gather them while they are still intact and perhaps, spray them with hairspray, to prevent their further ripening. Since, left alone, cattails multiply rapidly and their tangled roots gather silt which can eventually alter a shoreline, cattail spikes can be gathered without qualms.

Trees and Shrubs: Many species of evergreen and deciduous trees shade the edges of West Harbor Pond. What's exciting to find are such BIG trees. There are white pines and hemlocks which must have been growing there before Campbell's Cove was dammed in the 1890s, creating the fresh-water spring fed pond where there had been a brackish, tide-influenced cove.

The shrub which we found of greatest interest is sweet gale, *myrica gale*—because it was new to us. Its cousin, bayberry, grows nearby. Both have fragrant leaves; those of sweet gale are light in texture, whereas bayberry leaves seem leathery.

Ferns: From crevices in the big boulders hang polypody ferns, and in damp grassy spots are the twisted fronds of marsh fern. And, with its roots actually in the water, is the lovely royal flowering fern.

Animal Life: If the sun is shining, turtles are out on logs, enjoying it. They are probably painted turtles but they always slide into the water before we can examine the design on their backs. Frogs go kerplunk into the pond when your bow touches the shore.

We've seen and heard kingfishers, phoebes, tree swallows, herring, and black gulls. Occasionally a lone, immature loon cruises the water. There are great blue heron there and among the cattails, the little green heron. Red-winged blackbirds nest in these tangles. There are mallard ducks which have become tame, and, in the cove we have seen wild ducks of one kind or another.

In shallow water when the light is right, you can see lots of young fish. There must be some big ones in the deeper water. I'm told there are lots of bass and some lake trout in West Harbor Pond.

People who live at the pond say they've seen moose there in former years. Occasionally an otter is observed. This fresh-water mammal likes a home range of about 15 miles, including a chain of lakes, preferably connected by water.

I've only touched on the most obvious features of this

lovely body of water. Long may its water and shores remain a proper habitat for wild plants, wild creatures, and for people.

Can you understand why the canoe is my favorite of all vehicles?

July 11, 1985

AVIAN HELICOPTERS

The ruby-throated hummingbird arrives from Central America in time to drink the very first nectar that Maine has to offer. Although it is usually our hybrid azalea plant on which we first spy it, this year it was sipping from a daffodil! That was on Friday, the thirteenth—lucky day for us. We had seen it earlier than that and sometimes we learn that some of them had been flying about inside the Boothbay Region Greenhouses a full week before they were seen in gardens. The rubythroats will be with us all summer and they will be among the very last of the migrants to depart for the southland in autumn. We have seen them sipping nectar from our nasturtiums as late as early November. They are so beautiful! All the colors of the rainbow seem to be caught in their feathers when the sun is shining. Will Curtis (of WPBN Radio's Bed and Breakfast program, *That is the Nature of Things*) calls that plumage "refulgent." Synonyms for that adjective are given as shining, radiant, glowing. Yes, the hummingbird's plumage is refulgent. Synonyms for that adjective are given as shining, radiant, glowing. Yes, the hummingbird's plumage is refulgent.

World wide, there are more than three hundred species of hummingbirds. Of these, only thirteen breed in continental United States and our ruby-throat is the family's sole representative east of the Mississippi River. However, within the eastern states it is widely distributed and breeds from the Gulf of St. Lawrence to the Gulf of Mexico and has even been reported as far north as Hudson Bay.

These diminutive creatures can fly not only with extreme speed, but backwards and sidewards and even upside down, as well as forward! They can hover with wings in rapid vibration while the body is motionless. They can adjust level upwards or downwards at will. They can feed, hovering with the body tilted at various angles with the bill directed either vertically or horizontally! Furthermore the

migration of the hummingbird involves a sustained flight of the 500 miles across the Gulf of Mexico from Louisiana to Yucatan.

These superlative flying accomplishments are possible principally because of two factors unique to hummingbirds. One is the diet, the other is wing structure. The diet controls energy intake; the wing structure controls energy output. In his magnificent book, *Hummingbirds,* Crawford H. Greenawalt writes, "Perhaps the most extraordinary thing about the hummingbird is its power plant." This little bird's metabolism is the highest of any known warm-blooded animal. An enormous degree of energy is required to maintain the body temperature of so tiny a creature and to support the rapid wing activity. The hummingbird derives its quick energy as we do—through intake of sugar. Normally the sugar is supplied by the nectar of flowers—of which the favorites are the tubular ones like the azaleas, the trumpet vine, honeysuckles, columbine, foxglove, beebalm, nasturtium, salvia. There are many more. The color red seems to have a special attraction. It has been determined that a hummingbird consumes at least half its weight in sugar each day. But sugar alone is not enough.

When it feeds naturally, a hummingbird also devours tiny insects which of course provide protein, minerals, vitamins, and roughage. Although very small, these supplements are vital to the bird. Hummingbird feeders are all right for bringing the pretty creatures within easy sight, but they should not be a hummingbird's primary source of food. Besides, it is an even prettier sight to watch the birds probe the deep corollas of their favorite flowers.

A hummingbird's strong shoulder muscles and very supple shoulder joints permit axial rotation of about 180° and movement in all directions. The "hand" of the wing has more flight feathers than the "arm" has secondary feathers. With other birds the reverse is true. Most birds can secure lift and propulsion from the downstroke only; hummingbirds generate power with the upstroke also, thus achieving about twice the power per wingbeat.

Even so, this little bundle of energy requires devices for conservation of that energy. We see the bird when it is active—but it does perch, for as long as a half-hour at a time and for as much as 82 percent of the nighttime. At night it can slip into a torpid condition which lowers the body temperature from the daytime norm of from approximately 102° to 108° to almost that of the surrounding air. The condition is called "noctivation". The bird does not always noctivate, but in hotter climates than ours it often does. The bird's health, its present state of nourishment, and 'perhaps...its emotional state' (Alexander Skutch) all influence whether or not a hummingbird will noctivate. It's like a short-term hibernation. However, we are told, females do not noctivate—their body heat must be maintained for the successful development of the eggs and chicks.

You have to have bright eyes to discover the location of the nest which you know can't be far away from your garden. A tiny cup is daintily but strongly fashioned of felted plant fibers and fern scales, insulated with moss and lichen, lined with down (dandelion, for instance), and secured with spider web. It is a safe and inconspicuous nursery. Mother ruby throat has done all of the work involved. The male is a promiscuous philanderer, mating with several females throughout the season and assuming none of the chores. Sorry, but that's the way it is!

One year, when we knew a hummingbird nest must be nearby, we offered a prize to whichever of our children could discover its location. Sure enough, the hummingbird's secret was learned. "Mom! I found the nest!" was the excited announcement. The prize was a nature game which they all had fun with. That tiny nest was on a branch of red oak tree, about fifteen feet above the ground and looked, from our door, like nothing more than a scar on the bark of a branch. Our daughter had had to follow, with her eyes, the female as she made many trips from the beautybush into the tree. Feeding is by regurgitation; those who have witnessed the process say it seems as if the chicks would be pierced by her long bill as she pumps food into the tiny throats.

A friend wrote of an experience which had thrilled her. "A hummingbird was perched motionless on a thin dead snag. The long bill was silhouetted against the blue sky and the sun hit the throat just right to glow a bright red—perfect. With lots of time any half-cut photographer, could have taken many shots and switched all the lenses he had.."

May 26, 1988

KEEPING TRACK OF TAMI

Chipmunks, of all small, wild animals in our part of New England, are probably the most appealing to humans. We admire their industry and chuckle at their over-stuffed pouches, especially in autumn—and they're pretty!

One year we kept progress notes on a young chipmunk which first appeared on our deck with its mother on June 7th in the late afternoon. Not knowing whether it was a male or a female, we called this chipmunk "Tami". The scientific name for the eastern chipmunk is *tamias striatus*. *Tamais* means "steward" and a steward is one who stores and looks after provisions, and *striatus* means "striped". Very apt!

Tami was beautifully pillaged, nearly like an adult. The rusty tones were perhaps a bit brighter. The young chipmunk was approximately two-thirds the length of the mother; his tail was shorter and more thinly furred. Most notable was the pointed nose. Tami nibbled readily at seeds strewn on the deck but did not seem to stash a supply in his cheek pouches. The mother was the first to leave the deck.

The next afternoon at about the same time we saw them both again, nibbling from seeds at opposite sides of the deck. When the youngster approached the mother, she chased it. We didn't see them together after that but we did see young chipmunks eating there at the same time, quite independent of each other. They were undoubtedly littermates.

Tami grew rapidly during the next week. Although still slender, he was about as long as his mother, but his tail was still more sparsely furred than hers. We believe that June seventh was his first adventure outside the burrow in which he had spent his infancy along with his littermates (from two to as many as eight). This first trip could hardly have been earlier. Male and female chipmunks spend the winter in separate burrows. Often it's mid-March before they venture out for a change of diet and some welcome exercise. Mating, in northeastern states, is in April. If for Tami's parents that occurred on April first, allowing for the gestation period of 31 days, Tami and his littermates were born on May second.

They were blind and naked, warmed by their closeness to each other and to their mother whose milk they suckled. During the lovely weeks of May, when arbutus and trout lily and trilliums opened their buds, Tami and his brothers and sisters, remained in the dark underground nest, growing and becoming stronger each day but blind until May 27th. Yes, for chipmunks, 25 days must elapse between birth and eye-opening. An enforced safety plan?

But, apparently, the babies can then see immediately even in that darkness. Tami now wants to move about; his legs are stronger and his fur is thicker. He wants to find out about all sorts of things. Inquisitive, he explores the various galleries of the burrow. He finds a mound of acorns and another of hazelnuts and, I'm positive, one of sunflower seeds! While still underground, he learns to manipulate these objects in his facile, tiny forepaws and how to procure the kernels of the nuts and seeds. He experiments with the use of his pouches, but as yet he has no need to hoard. Tumbling and wrestling with his littermates strengthen his muscles and the tasting of the stored nuts release him from dependence upon his mother's milk. As he wanders about the burrow, new food smells and fragrances come to his nostrils. He knows he must leave the burrow.

For chipmunks, there is no post-nest care as there is with most birds. Once they leave the nest they are on their own. One wonders, did the mother lead Tami, perhaps the most precocious in that litter and the first to leave the subterranean home, to an easily obtained first outside meal?

Since Tami is a vegetarian, there's a lot of food available to him right now. But almost immediately he must prepare his own burrow in which to sleep and seek refuge from those who would consider him a good meal (a hawk, mink, fox, cat, and the greatest threat of all, a weasel). He must construct that burrow and that project will require a great amount of labor and of stored chipmunk wisdom. It must have several chambers below frostline—some for food storage, a sleeping room, a latrine. A female chipmunk also prepares a grass-lined "nest". When the inside is completed to Tami's satisfaction, he must go back to what had been his entrance, plug it well with the excavated earth, and hide the evidence with leaves, twigs, etc. What was the exit is now the entrance and this is usually very obscure. Tami may also have one or more escape-holes for convenience and safety.

We are told that often in late summer chipmunks seem to "sing" and to answer each other. Alan Devoe, author of *The World of a Chipmunk,* has said, "Animal life, even the least and littlest, like Tamias', has in it the element of a simple primal exultation."

June 5, 1997

BLOSSOMS AT 80 FEET

It grows in all of Maine's 16 counties, often borders well-traveled roads, yet we pass it by unnoticed except in these late spring and early summer weeks when its pendant clusters of fragrant white blossoms demand our attention. I'm referring to the black locust tree, *robinia pseudo-acacia*.

There's a row of these trees on Route 27, north of the Edgecomb Town Hall. Also, Route 28 in Dresden, both north and south of the Pownalborough Courthouse, has a fine display of black locusts. And they grow in many other Lincoln County locations.

Although this is a native American tree, its original range did not extend into Maine. Now it is naturalized in all of the eastern states and in parts of the west as well. Furthermore, it was introduced into Europe as early as 1636 by Jean Robin (herbalist to Henry IV of France) or possibly by Jean's son, Vespasien, probably from Louisiana. The tree's generic name, *robinia*, honors these herbalists. "Toward the end of the 18th century in Europe the growing of black locust became a rage." (Donald Cultross Peattie, *A Natural History of Trees*.)

What features did the black locust tree possess which so appealed to the Europeans? Its wood is extremely hard and very durable. Used in boat construction, treenails of locust wood were strong, long-lived, unexcelled by any other known material for that purpose.

The tree's tough, weather-resistant wood was also the reason for its being widely planted throughout the northeast and adjacent Canada. It was proven to be especially suitable for fenceposts and wagonwheel hubs, as well as the treenails with which to pin ship timbers together. Still earlier these trees served an extremely valuable service. Our first colonists from England did not build log cabins for their first dwellings. In fact, they didn't understand log cabin construction until Scandinavians and Germans arrived in America. One hundred years after the founding of Jamestown, the British naturalist, Mark Catesby, wrote, "Being obliged to run up with all the expedition possible such little houses as might serve them to dwell in, till they could find leisure to build larger and more convenient ones, they erected each of their little hovels on four only of these trees (the locust-tree of Virginia), pitched into the ground to support the four corners; many of these posts are yet standing, and not only the parts underground, but likewise those above, still perfectly sound."

In this century, however, the principal industrial use of the wood of the black locust tree is for insulator pins on transmission line cross-arms. Twenty-five million such pins were made in a single recent year—requiring 18,000 cords of wood!

Peattie, in the book mentioned above, gives a lovely description of the black locust tree's potential. "Under any name, this tree is impressive, when it grows to a soldierly 80 feet, the trunk 3 or 4 feet thick and the topmost branches often spreading the ferny foliage high above the surrounding trees. When the locust flowers, in the late spring, its pendant spikes of honey-sweet blossoms look as though some white wisteria had climbed in the stalwart tree and let down fragrant tassels of bloom." However, locust boards are almost unknown, principally because the locust borer beetle, *cyllene robina*, is so devastating here in America. "It is almost universal and no measures of control have had any effect" (Peattie, writing in 1950). However, there is a variety of the black locust tree, known as "shipmast locust" which seems to be resistant (or undesirable) to that beetle. The Conservation Commission of West Virginia was working toward the propagation of a beetle-free strain of this tree. Peattie closed his essay on the black locust tree with these words: "...If ever we come to our senses and start planting and growing our valuable hardwoods instead of cutting them down faster than they can be replaced, shipmast locust might be one of the first varieties on which to concentrate."

Now, let's refocus our attention on the locust tree's delightful blossoms, with their appeal to our eyes, our noses, and our tastebuds. *Pennsylvania German Cookery* (by Ann Hark and Preston A Barba, 1950) includes a recipe for "Black Locust Blossom Fritters".

Prepare a batter made from 2 well beaten eggs, 1 cup milk, 1/2 t. salt, 2 cups flour. Beat until smooth. Wash the racemes of native black locust tree when in full blossom and heavy in honey and fragrance. Break them in small parts and dip into the batter. Fry in deep hot fat, 360°F. for about three minutes or until a golden brown. Toss the fritters in a brown paper bag containing some powdered sugar. "Taste and fragrance not of this earth! Poetry reduced to food!" We find ourselves wondering if dear Dr. and Mrs. Barba have prepared this delicacy for the angels in heaven!

And Euell Gibbons, in *Stalking the Healthful Herbs*, gives his own version of locust blossom fritters and he tells us how to extract the perfume of the flowers to be stored in vials for later use. He describes the scent of the black locust as "sweet school-girlish fragrance."

BLACK LOCUST FRITTERS

2 eggs, well beaten
1 cup milk
1/2 tsp. salt
2 cups flour

Racemes of native black locust trees, in full blossom, heavy in honey & fragrance (also works with elder-flower blossoms.)

Combine milk and eggs and beat till foamy. Add salt. Stir into flour and beat until a smooth batter results. Wash the racemes of native black locust tree. Break them in small parts and dip into the batter. Fry in deep hot fat, 360°F. for about three minutes or until a golden brown. Toss the fritters in a brown paper bag containing some powdered sugar. Eat while hot.

July 1, 1993

MYSTICAL MOTHS

Queries from two readers prompt today's focus on moths.

"Is it rare for there to be a luna moth in Maine? We picked up a dead one on Sawyer's Island this week—but we've never seen one here before."

"What is it that hovers over the flowers in my garden? The wings beat rapidly—but it's not a hummingbird, nor is it a bumble-bee."

The quick answer to query one is that, yes, luna moths are unusual in Maine—for the very simple reason that the food-trees for its caterpillars are absent or uncommon this far north.

The larvae of most moths, and butterflies, are very selective in their eating habits. "Most caterpillars eat only one kind of leaves. They will starve to death if given the wrong kind of food." (*The Junior Book of Insects* by Edwin Way Teale, Dutton, 1939). The luna caterpillar eats the leaves of sweet gum, persimmon, walnut, and hickory trees. Neither sweet gum nor persimmon grow in Maine. The nut trees, shagbark hickory and white walnut (butternut) do occur "locally in southern Maine on moist, but well-drained soil." (*Forest Trees of Maine*, Maine Forest Service, 1981). There can, of course, be a shagbark hickory tree or a butternut tree, perhaps purposely planted near the place the luna was found. Black walnut trees have been introduced in a few places in Maine. I've seen only one *juglans nigra* during our 21 years in Maine. So, yes, it was indeed unusual to find the body of an adult luna moth on Sawyer's Island.

The sighting of the insect hovering over garden flowers in a manner suggesting a hummingbird or a bumblebee can be answered with these few words: "You saw a moth, a member of the sphinx family, sometimes called 'clearwinged sphinx' and more often, 'hummingbird moth'". But that statement is only a flat fact whereas to observe that little insect with its wings vibrating so rapidly that we see only a blur, is really quite a thrill. What the creature is doing—but we'd have to have a movie running at slow-motion to see that the process is of drinking nectar and incidentally pollinating the flower! This little moth is an exception to the general rule that moths are night-fliers; butterflies are day-fliers. Sphinx moths have tongues even longer than their bodies and although they are most often seen flying about the garden, sipping flowers at dusk, especially on hot evenings, they are sometimes also seen in the bright sun of mid-day.

The beautiful, big, more leisurely-flying luna moth and the high-intensity, small, darting hummingbird moth are adults in two different families of moths (of which there are 8,800 species in 75 families!). Since most moths are night-fliers, we are much more familiar with adult butterflies, of which there are only five families with 700 species in the USA.

Butterflies and moths comprise the order of insects known as *lepidoptera*. For a clear and concise description of the features of these two groups I think that *Insects* by Zim and Cottam, a *Golden Nature Guide* paperback, is excellent. I recommend that you own it, especially if you have children whose curiosity about the natural world you want to encourage.

All moths and butterflies have four stages in their life cycles—egg, larva, pupa, adult. Let's follow the beautiful luna moth through its development. A cluster of fertilized eggs is deposited on an acceptable food-plant. These will hatch in approximately 10-12 days into tiny but ravenous larvae. The caterpillars eat the leaf-tissue, first as a group, later singly, and are constantly growing. Especially while they are small many of them are eaten by birds and by other insects. As they grow, shedding their skin several times, the pale green caterpillars also develop rows of bright red tubercles—which may serve to frighten potential predators which would relish a juicy morsel. When the larva have completed their eating stage, they have attained a size of approximately 3 inches. They becomes inactive; their skin color changes to a pinkish tone; they are ready to pupate.

Although other silkworms spin cocoons which they attach to the food-tree, the luna larva drops to the ground, where it spins a thin cocoon between leaves. It's a papery enclosure which rattles when you handle it. In Pennsylvania, my father-in-law used to carefully poke among the leaves under his hickory nut tree and would sometimes find a luna cocoon to show our daughter.

Within the cocoon, over the winter, the pupa miraculously is transformed into a very beautiful moth. It has large green wings which have purplish borders and long, ribbon-like tails. Its antennae are conspicuously feathered. It has only a few days to live during which it will not eat but will fly in the darkness and find a mate. The female will then deposit eggs on its nearest food plant. The cycle commences again. Metamorphosis is complete.

July 7, 1994

SUMMER'S HIGHLIGHT

This summer's highlight for us was having our two grand-children with us at Baxter Park for four days in late July. This was Jeff's sixth stay at Kidney Pond, the first having been in 1979 when he was seven years old. Now he's fifteen. Anya is six-and-a half and it was her first Baxter Park experience. It's a half-day drive from our home. We were assigned to Carter's Lodge which is ideal for two adults and two children, affording family privacy. It faces Sentinel Mountain, and has its own dock and swimming area.

Jeff and Anya were soon cooling off in the pond. Jeff is a strong swimmer; Anya is a learner. "I can swim under water, but not on top." There was time, too for the cousins to use the canoe that first afternoon. By now Jeff is a competent canoeist. At first he received a good deal of back-splash from his bow-paddler but he was a good instructor. By the third day Anya was feeling at ease in the canoe and handling her short paddle properly. Jeff always paddled to the lodge for meals. "Of course. Where else can you go where you can canoe to your breakfast?"

Blessed with wonderful weather, our four days included an expedition to Big Niagara which entails crossing both Kidney and Lily Pad ponds and hiking the short trails that link them. Anya had her introduction to water-sliding at the base of Big Niagara.

There were walks to The Point and to The Bench. Jeff took Anya by canoe into the outlet to see the beaver lodge and dam. She actually saw a beaver swimming and she learned to recognize a beaver-chewed stick. We watched the graceful loons and were happy to see that their twin babies had grown to almost adult size. The loonlets took short dives but still preferred to have their food caught and served by their parents. That family of four was usually together.

There was a hike to Draper Pond; there were evenings

cool enough to be glad for a fire in the cabin's wood-stove while we played a game together. Anya made friends with a chipmunk and discovered its burrow entrance. On the morning of our last full day, we walked a lovely stretch of the Appalachian Trail, skirting Tracy, Grassy, and Elbow Ponds.

Anya is a child who loves animals. Seeing six moose during her first trip into Maine's north woods was, it seems, her most memorable and cherished experience. Over the phone, she told her father, "Daddy, I saw SIX moose! Two were eating cow-lilies in the outlet. And one day we saw a mother moose and she had two calves with her! The very last day there was a young bull, with velvety horns—over near the lodge."

Jeff had enjoyed introducing Anya to some of his favorite places and he had been generous and patient when helping her with paddling techniques. But we sensed that for him this Baxter Park experience should include a challenge—something on his own level. He yearned to climb Doubletop. Doubletop is Kidney Pond's own mountain. The sight of it greets every visitor as we cross the Nesowadnehunk Stream to enter the Kidney Pond Road. From the pond it looms as dramatic background for the lodge. Jeff had seen the sign for the trail to its summit—"3.9 miles to S. Peak; 4.1 miles to N. Peak." "I could do it in an afternoon. I know I could." Should we allow him to do it—alone? My wonderful camp director, Mary J. Littlefield, used to say, "For a teenager a good game or other physical activity should have an element of danger and a degree of safety. To climb Double Top, solo, certainly presented the element of danger. What about safety?

Jeff was in top physical condition. An Eagle Boy Scout, he had, with his troop, climbed most of the peaks in the Presidential Range of the White Mountains. He said to John, "Pa, I'll wear my watch and when half my time is gone. I'll turn around." We trusted him. And we knew that the camp could quickly summon emergency help from the ranger station. Jeff quickly prepared himself—comfortable hiking shoes, a canteen of water, a light backpack containing gloves, a jacket, a First Aid Kit. John drove him to the start of the trail where they agreed to meet at 5:30. The time was then 1:30.

Imagine our surprise to have him walk into our cabin at 4:15, having attained both the north and south summits! By walking back to the cabin, he had added another one-half mile, making his round-trip a total of eight and one-half miles. It's a stiff climb. From the bridge it appears to be straight up; the top is bare, vertical rock. There were blow-downs to bushwhack around. Doubletop's elevation is 3,488 feet. Kidney Pond's is 1,088 feet. Jeff had climbed 2,437 feet in 2 and three-quarter hours. He had met his challenge well. Of course, he paddled to his dinner.

Back in Boothbay we stopped for raspberries. Anya spoke up: "Grandmama, may I please make the dessert tonight? I have a good recipe." "What ingredients will you need, Anya?" "Raspberries, sugar and the kind of whipped cream you squirt from a can." So, after our main meal was eaten, I pulled out the lower table in the kitchen and placed on it a bowl of washed and sugared raspberries, a spoon, and a can of aerated whipping cream. I returned to the dining room. Soon Anya strode in proudly, went straight to Jeff and plunked in front of him a gorgeous concoction. "Here, Jeff. Yours is DOUBLETOP." Sure enough, there were twin peaks atop a red and white mountain!

Aug. 27, 1987

OUR WILD CANARY

The American goldfinch is, indeed, a gregarious bird, recognizable, at least in summer plumage, to almost everyone. Social and friendly, they choose our gardens, our fields, our roadsides, and our edges of woodlands in which to nest, or so it seems, to frolic.

With characteristic, undulating flight they dip and swerve, dozens of them together, twittering and singing on the wing, justifying the bird's nickname "wild canary". It mystifies us as to how it was ever given the scientific name *spinus tristis* which translates as "the sad linnet" (from the Greek *spinus* which refers to linnet or finch, and from the Latin *tristis* meaning sad). We would rename our wild canary *spinus hilaris* which would translate as "the merry linnet" or "the blythe finch"—or, if we dared to play with the generic name, we could call him *carduelis hiraris*.

The European goldfinch has the generic name *carduelis* which is derived from the Latin *carduus* which means "thistle". The American and the European goldfinches are very close biologically both in appearance and in behavior. The principal apparent distinctions being that the European goldfinch has a bright red facial patch and is slightly larger. German people call the European goldfinch *distelfink* meaning "thistle finch" and our Pennsylvania German settlers promptly dubbed our American goldfinch with the same name. And, very apt it is since the bird depends heavily upon the roadside thistles for both food and nesting material.

In fact, no self-respecting pair of *distelfinks* would think of providing their babies with anything less comfortable than a nest padded and insulated with plantdown, preferably that of one of the thistles. But this material is not available to them until the summer season is well along, which is one big reason why the goldfinch is the last of the songbirds to get down to the business of rearing a family. In

Birds of the Eastern Forest John A. Livingston points out that "it takes them about twice as long to build a nest in July as it does in August, when the thistles, milkweed, dandelions, and others are at their best." Nor would the parents settle for anything less than the perfect formula for infant goldfinches, which has been described as "a white viscid mass" composed of regurgitated, partially digested seeds—of thistle, chicory, dandelion, ragweed, and a score of other plants, most of which are not in seed until summer is well advanced.

The cup-shaped nest may have a wide variety of structural material. The female apparently builds it alone. She usually starts "from scratch" but she is willing to use an abandoned red-wing blackbird's nest as a base. She will also dismantle

old nests of various songbirds such as northern oriole or yellow warbler to use the second-hand material in her own nest which she places in the fork of a blackberry bush, tree sapling or other plant, usually within five feet of the ground but sometimes as high as thirty feet. But whether the foundation of the nursery is of new or recycled material, the lining of thistledown is new and so intricately woven that it is actually waterproof. The edges of the cradle are usually bound with the strong, fine webbing spun by spiders or caterpillars and they are strengthened with long plant fibers. It's a very special nest!

Once the female is satisfied with the little home she lays in it four, five, or six pale-blue eggs, and on these she sits closely, very seldom leaving the nest during the entire incubation period of from twelve to fourteen days. During this stretch she is fed by her mate with a pabulum similar to the concoction which later both parents bring to the babies for the eleven to fourteen days that they are nestlings.

In the old (1920) but delightful book, *Bird Neighbors* by Neltje Blanchan, the author comments that "The cares evolving from the four to six pale-blue eggs will suffice to quiet the father's song for the winter by the first of September, and fade all the glory out of his shining coat." That's a rather fanciful explanation but, whatever the reason, it's a fact that in autumn and winter the adult male has plumage almost as muted as that of his mate and offspring. You have to look closely and critically to discern, in early winter, that he has a vaguely yellow shoulder-patch and that the black is blacker and the white whiter in his wings and tail than in those of the female. "One thing I cannot convince some persons," wrote one of my readers, "is that the male goldfinches change color in winter. They look, in color, like miniature female evening grosbeaks—but when they fly one knows what they are."

As winter moves into spring, the weed seeds of the fields become more scarce. The goldfinches move, then, to where they can find alder and birch seeds, some of which are held on those trees in their catkins throughout the winter. It's in late winter and early spring, too, that these wild canaries come to the feeders where, although they prefer the thistle seed which many of us offer in tubular containers, they also like to feast on millet, hemp, and sunflower seeds. Then we are in for a treat, for we can observe the transformation of the males. An olive-colored fellow in January, almost indistinguishable from the female and juvenile birds, he will, at first very subtly and later much more abruptly, molt his drab feathers, revealing the new, bright yellow ones. Suddenly, it seems, he's in full spring dress, his olive top-knot replaced by a jet-black one, his black tail and wings emphasizing the yellow of his general plumage. He's our merry goldfinch again, our distelfink, ready to sing and cavort in a flock of dozens of his own kind until summer is well under way.

Now, summer is indeed, well under way! Dandelion fluff is on the breeze; soon there will be thistle and milkweed down. Within a very short time the goldfinches will be pairing, selecting territory, and commencing nest construction. Only careful observation will let us know just when this activity begins and, if we're very lucky, where the unique nursery is located.

July 18, 1985

GRACE AND STRENGTH

Here in coastal Maine herring gulls are part of our life. We see and hear them every day. It seems incredible now, when this gull seems to be the most common water bird along our shores, that at one time its numbers were reduced to just one colony on the entire Atlantic Coast. This depletion was a direct result of the craze, in the late 1800s and early 1900s, for plumes and feathers as millinery adornment. Thanks to President Theodore Roosevelt, to the persuasive writings of John Muir and John Burroughs, and to the work of the newly incorporated "National Association of Audubon Societies for the Protection of Wild Birds and Animals" (1905), it became embarrassing, rather than popular, to wear a hat decorated with a plume, a wing or a tail. The Weeks-McLean Act was passed in 1913. It was the first effective law protecting migratory birds.

Today, this gull's breeding range along the Atlantic Coast extends from Labrador to at least as far south as North Carolina. It also nests in Alaska and along Canada's Pacific Coast as well as on the shores and islands of many lakes in our northern states and southern Canada. As they soar over the ocean they are beautiful; as one drops a clam onto a ledge and then retrieves the tasty morsel we admire the bird's intelligence. It's true that when we see them eating garbage (as they did regularly while we had open dumps), we find the sight repulsive. Yet its willingness to scavenge, to eat our waste, should also command our admiration —and thanks. Our own pursuits have reduced the quantity of small fish and mollusks available to gulls. So they follow the fishing boats into shore and eat the discarded waste as it is tossed into the water. Their scavenging habits, although unpleasant to witness, are of very definite value to humans. And they are so beautiful!

Herring gulls frequently nest in colonies, often on a cliff, perhaps on the edge of an island. However like most successful species, herring gulls will settle for second best when they can't have their first choice of either habitat or food. They will breed in sand dunes, on grass, on fresh water inland lakes, on boughs of evergreen trees, and even on rooftops!

In each active herring gull's nest, composed of seaweed, grass, and other plant material, two or three or even up to five eggs are laid, each about the size of a chicken egg. They will be relatively inconspicuous with a muted background color and they will be laid at intervals of two or three days, with incubation starting with the first egg. Therefore, they will hatch at two or three day intervals, also.

A few years ago, we were walking along a Monhegan Island trail which led us close to a cliff edge. We overtook a party of hikers and there was obvious excitement. Herring gulls were making a big fuss and we heard a man call, "Don't get too close!" and "Mary, be careful!" and "Do come back!" He turned, explaining, "Mary is so loving. She'd never hurt them, but the gulls don't know that!" A dozen or so of the big gulls swooped menacingly over the young woman (perhaps 18 or 19 years old) who, as she returned to the trail, yelled, elatedly, "But Dad, I'd never seen a gull's nest before! I saw a tiny, fluffy baby and I saw eggs in the nest too." Mary was a very satisfied person at that point. She had been lucky as well as adventurous—but a peck on the head by an alarmed gull could have really hurt her. I do not recommend her pursuit to you!

If the fluffy chick that Mary saw had hatched that very day, the egg would probably have been laid 25 or so days earlier. If there were three eggs in the clutch, laid at two-day intervals, the second chick to hatch from the egg would be sharing the nest with an older and stronger sibling and, two days later, with a younger, weaker brother or sister. This creates a very demanding situation for the parent gulls. The male had shared with his mate the chore of incubation, with the female spending more time on the nest. Once the babies are hatched both parents tend them with full-time devotion.

That's a really busy and hazardous time for the gull family; the down-covered hatchling is semi-precocial. Its eyes are open but it does require a few days of brooding— protection from sun, rain, and predators. And it needs to be fed for a while (with food regurgitated by the parents). It will be six weeks before the nestling will fly. So that nestful of chicks with staggered ages and strengths presents gull parents with a real challenge. Perhaps there are still one or two eggs to be kept warm and safe! The youngsters soon become adept at picking up their own food but for quite some time they will beg from their parents or any other adult in the colony. They may be rewarded with food—or with a disciplinary peck on the head!

In *The Long-Shadowed Forest,* Helen Hoover writes of the beauty of a herring gull on a northern Minnesota lake: "I do not believe that any language has words adequate to portray their fluid motion, their strength and grace, the accuracy of their bankings and turnings—their landings, when they hang motionless on curved wings, then drop, without splash and with wings folding, onto the water."

July 21, 1994

MARVELOUS MALLOWS

Our mini-meadow, an unmowed back yard, is colorful right now as we expect it to be until frost comes. Presently abloom are ox-eye daisies, black-eyed susans, and musk mallows. From the kitchen window there's a foreground of yellow day-lilies. Wild roses and a woodpile provide the background. We have no lawnmower but John does use a weedwhacker enough that we can walk comfortably between the clumps of flowers. Clovers and ferns and deptford pinks crowd in where they can. We have wildflower bouquets around the house and at our front door. This week our dining-table's centerpiece is composed of the pretty soft-pink blossoms of the musk mallow and sprigs of sweet fern.

Today we'll feature the musk mallow and other members of the mallow family.

To begin with, we must acknowledge that this is not a native North American wildflower. It and some of its relatives were introduced from Europe and have spread from old gardens and are now known as "introduced and naturalized wildflowers."

Eight representatives of the *malvaceae* grow in Maine, all of them introduced from Europe. Of the eight, only musk mallow is known to grow in all sixteen of our counties. It is also known as common mallow. This species is now abundant from Newfoundland throughout most of the northeast, brightening fields and roadsides. Another well known mallow is the small-flowered "cheeses".

In our case, we admired musk mallow where it grew at the doorway of a friend in Edgecomb. She promptly dug a clump of it for us. It seems to be happy where we put it. It spreads but is readily controlled; its seeds take root if we toss some where we'd like more plants to grow. As a cutting flower, it has many attributes. Its pretty, soft-pink petals harmonize with other flowers and they hold up well in water.

Like other mallows, its pithy stems are efficient conductors of moisture.

Even if musk mallow were the sole representative of the relatively small mallow family, we'd enjoy and respect it. But no, it has distinguished relatives.

"The most important member of the mallow family is the cotton plant. The down upon its seeds makes all our cotton fabrics." (Alice M. Dowd in *Our Common Wildflowers* which she prepared for her school children and which was published in 1906.)

Six decades later, in 1965, the eminent botanist, Harold William Rickert, wrote of the mallows in his fine, multi-volumed work, *Wild Flowers of the United States.*"It is not a large family but has contributed what is certainly one of the world's most important crops." Cotton continues to be of great intrinsic value to the human race. Perhaps we appreciate it most during a heat wave!

Other mallows were of importance to us over shorter periods of time. The roots of all mallows are to some degree *mucilaginous*, those of the marsh mallow especially so. The popular confection named for it (marshmallow) was prepared with the thickened juice of the roots of this plant and sugar. A Greek physician, as early as the first-century A.D., had devoted himself to the study of plants for healing. His treatise was translated into English in 1655. In it he listed dozens of complaints for which marsh mallow was a remedy and wrote that its root "also doth thicken water being mixed when it is beaten small." Marshmallows, today, are made with corn syrup and gelatin.

Another mallow, velvet-leaf, its origin Asia, was brought to America in 1750 from England with the plan of cultivating it for use in bags, cordage and ropes. Here it is called American hemp or American jute. But that project failed and the plant is considered a weed detrimental to maize and soy beans...The vegetable okra, grown in the south, provides the popular ingredient for chicken gumbo soup. The plant, botanically, is known as *hibiscus esculetus*; the part used is the young fruit.

Except for cotton and okra, the many, many uses our ancestors found for mallows are now relegated to the category of "lore," although some of them are included in modern medicines.

Horticulturists, however, have developed beautiful strains of hollyhocks and of hibiscus and of rose of sharon, all of them mallows, adding beauty to gardens in many parts of our country.

We're happy to have the common musk mallow to look at from our kitchen window and to have its blossoms grace our home.

July 20, 1995

THE BOTTLE CLUB

It has become a happy custom for us to spend several weeks at Kidney Pond Camps each year. The mountains—Katahdin, OJI, Squaw's Bosom, Doubletop—and the ponds they rim— Kidney, Lily Pad, Draper, the Rockies, Celia—seem, by now, to belong to us. And they do—in two ways. Baxter Park belongs "to the people of Maine", the far-sighted gift of Percival Proctor Baxter. The other way is less tangible. They are "treasures of the humble heart" which we keep "in true possession, owning them by love." (Henry Van Dyke).

This year, our week was as enjoyable as always. Weather-wise, we experienced a little of everything—rain, sun, hail, wind, calm cool days, no black flies. We saw and heard the loons and the woodcock and the bittern. A pair of American mergansers and a pair of ring-necked ducks swam on Kidney Pond's outlet. We sniffed arbutus, saw a slope of painted trillium and noted that all wildflowers were almost a week later than usual to bloom. We walked to favorite places and paddled on favorite ponds, climaxing our stay with a trip to Big Niagara which involves paddling across Kidney Pond, walking a mile on woods trail, carrying paddles, safety-cushions and lunch, paddling across Lily Pad Pond, and then hiking the trail along Sourdnehunk Stream to the falls—which were very full, thunderous, and misty. Just before leaving Big Niagara campsite we had a meeting of "The Bottle Club". This was held around the handcrafted woods-table which stands on a needle-strewn ledge under big spruce trees and overlooks the falls. The feature of The Bottle Club is, of course, a bottle and its contents. But this is a bottle to which we add, not from which we take. Here's the story:

In the summer of 1980, we brought our grandson, Jeffrey and his mother, our daughter, Mary Liz to Kidney Pond Camps for a three-night, four-day stay. Jeff was eight years old and it was his second visit to this lovely part of Baxter

Park. The trip via canoe and trail to Big Niagara was the highlight of our time at camp. We lingered as long as we could and then we started back. As we walked along a path we'd taken many times before, Jeff noticed something gleaming and called it to our attention. We thought someone might have stashed some litter—glass or foil perhaps—so John reached for it.

It turned out to be a capped bottle which had once held wine but which now contained coiled pieces of paper (perhaps two dozen) and a pencil stub. Our curiosity aroused, we took it back to the table and removed a few of the coils. Each was a short record of a happy time at this very place. Each was dated and signed by several people. One of the first few we opened read something like this: "Anyone who finds this bottle may read our notes. Please add your own, sign your name(s), date it, and return it all to its hiding-place".

Well! What had we here? Fascinated, we read every note. Although they weren't read in order, the story was clear. Three generations of people, with two surnames (perhaps one, perhaps two families) had always included Big Niagara as a cherished part of their visits to Kidney Pond Camps. They called themselves the "Barnes-Rundle Clan" (not their true names). They played "mumblety-peg" after lunch, they had in-clan jokes and teasings. The signatures on the earliest note included one of a boy who might have been in first grade judging by the printed name. I think the date was 1959. The boy (Tom, we'll call him) would have been six or seven years old—a bit younger than Jeff was in 1980. After a few years the grandfather's signature was not included. One mentioned Tom as a college student and in a subsequent note Tom was in medical school. In a still later note a young lady had signed next to Tom's name and on the latest note in the bottle (probably 1979) those two young people had the same surname. The "Barnes-Rundle Clan" had a new member.

What fun! What a lovely way to make a record of "trips to our favorite place". We carefully recoiled the notes, returned them to the bottle and, with their pencil and a piece of paper torn from our lunchbag, wrote our own note to these members of the "Barnes-Rundle Clan". We knew we'd like these people. We restored the bottle to its hiding-place, concealing it well with an extra plug of moss so that no bottle-rim gleamed to reveal its presence.

This had been in late July. When we returned to Boothbay Harbor, Jeff said, "We ought to have our own bottle. It's such a great idea." So, around a mid-summer hearth-fire, we composed a note from the four of us, mentioning the high points of our all-too-short stay, and we signed it as members of "the Heyl-Bauer Clan." We found a bottle into which we dropped that first record and John and I were assigned the pleasant responsibility of taking "our bottle" to the falls, selecting a suitable, secret cache, and stashing the "Heyl-Bauer Clan" bottle in that recess.

It was September, 1980, when we hid the bottle containing that first midsummer note plus one written that very day. Friends were with us, so they signed it too. Each year since then there have been two and sometimes three notes added, and many friends, including Boothbay neighbors have signed the notes, adding remarks of their own. As far as we know the hideaway has not been detected.

Although we've never read any more Barnes-Rundle notes, we did remove their bottle last spring (1983), planning to just demonstrate to a friend how this Bottle Club had started. To our dismay, we realized that moisture had gotten in and many of the notes appeared to be damp. Our good friend, Miriam Schantz, was with us and she said, "I'm going to take this bottle back to camp. I'll dry out the notes and next week I'll return it and stash it carefully." We had to leave the next day; Miriam had another week.

Later, she told us that two or three days later she heard, in the dining-room, a familiar name, "Tom Rundle". Looking in that direction she saw a young couple and their baby. She approached Tom, ascertained his identity, and then told him she had "the bottle" in her cabin. They were grateful. Tom's wife said she'd copy the notes before returning them to the bottle and later, at home she'd type them—a record of 24 years of happy times at a beloved place. I believe that the youngest member of the Barnes-Rundle Clan was back-packed to Big Niagara later that week—and perhaps he (or maybe she) managed to make a personal mark on that latest note.

May 24, 1984

NIGHT FORAGERS

Grandchildren are not the only young creatures who, in this month of August, are exploring wet sandy beaches and tangles of rockweed at low tide. Handlike footprints, large and small, tell us that young raccoons are now accompanying their mothers on nightly forays which include saltwater habitats. The kits are now over three months old and they are becoming more and more adept at procuring their own food.

And what omnivorous appetites they have! Whatever berries are ripe they sample and, of all the wild berries, they seem to enjoy the tangy-sweet wineberries most of all. One night we made the mistake of leaving out some apricots which we had placed in the sun to ripen. It was an unplanned contribution to the fruit-cup course of a raccoon dinner! Along a brook or pondside they learn to catch small fish, frogs, insect larvae, freshwater mussels, and crayfish. So much for the freshwater-food cocktail; on the way to the beach they will stop to dig for nightcrawlers with their long, sensitive fingers and they'll pull rotten logs apart searching for grubs, lift stones for salamanders, and scratch in the sand for turtle eggs. At the beach and in tidepools, they find tiny soft-shelled crabs, shrimp, baby fish, and young mussels.

Raccoons do prefer to wash their food before eating it but motivation is almost surely comfort, not cleanliness. Mussels are gritty; many morsels are encaked with mud. Also, the raccoon seems not to have a ready flow of saliva; therefore water is a help when eating dry food...but corn? It's clean and sweet and juicy right where it is; no need to lug it to the brook! His craving for sweet corn and also his gourmet appreciation of tender chicken or duckling do not endear the raccoon to the owners of small corn patches or duck ponds.

This is the wild mammal who, more than any other, will adjust its lifestyle to a man-altered environment. Not only will he eat from our gardens, snitch food from the garbage can, dismantle bird-feeders so as to have access to the supply of sunflower seed or suet—he will even become friendly. If you choose to develop his trust, he'll actually eat from your hand. And the mother will bring her babies to you for a handout. This is a delight—but the raccoon is not readily disciplined and you may regret having encouraged it to accept you as a friend. I do not recommend it.

Adaptable as they are as to what they will eat and where they will hunt for food, they definitely prefer a den-tree for their shelter which is why we think of them as denizens of a deciduous woodland. When hard-pressed, a crevice in the rocks or even the space under a summer cottage may be used but that's "making do"; a hollow tree is better.

The raccoon is an expert climber. The adult can descend from a tall tree either backwards or forwards—although a young one always goes down backwards. Nevertheless, the raccoon is not a nest-builder and so several forces must have been at work over quite a long time before a tree can offer a suitable den. An injury from lightning or wind is what usually starts the making of a den-tree. Once rain and snow can reach unprotected, inner wood, there is decay. The rotting organic matter is fed upon by insects, including ants which in turn attract flickers who chop away in search of their favorite food. There may then be a sequence of tenancies in such a decaying tree.

In *Raccoons Are The Brightest People*, Sterling North

tells us that nuthatches were the first birds to be observed deepening a natural cavity. They were searching for grubs. This activity resulted in the hole being accepted by a pair of nesting bluebirds. Another season downy woodpeckers used the hollow; later the large hairy woodpeckers moved in and then the great pileated woodpeckers nested in it, each tenant enlarging the hole to suit its requirements. Since a pileated woodpecker's nest must measure almost twenty inches and since an adult raccoon, exclusive of the tail, measures from eighteen to twenty-eight inches, you can see that the cavity would not be nearly large enough to serve as a den-tree for raccoons. However, the tree observed by Mr. North served an interim season or two as a gray squirrel's cache for acorns.Then, probably ten years after the first occupancy of the hole, a female raccoon took up residence in it.

A female raccoon is only ten months old when she is ready to mate. By that time she has found her own den-tree and in early March or late April she receives visits from several males. (This is known by the numerous and slightly different-sized tracks under the den-tree.) She is fastidious and selective but finally accepts one suitor as her mate. He is at least one year older than herself. He dens up with her for a week or so and, sixty-three days after mating, her tiny kits, usually four of them and weighting only two to three ounces each, are born. Nursed in their safe den-tree, they grow rapidly and at the age of ten weeks are ready for the first descent to the ground and for lessons in food-procuring and self-protection.

Some reported observations indicate that although the polygamous male has had no contact with his family up to this time, he now rejoins the mother and assists her while the kits are so vulnerable. Man and his dogs are the greatest threats to their safety and a large owl or a fox will eat a baby raccoon if he can secure it. A male raccoon can put up a fierce and successful fight when he wants to.

At least through November and perhaps into mid-winter the coon family will stay together, not really hibernating when winter comes, but sleeping most of the time, safe in the den-tree during storms.

Has the child you love read Sterling North's *Rascal*? It's delightful.

Aug. 12, 1982

THE INDIAN-PIPE

We may have walked the same woodland trail just yesterday and so we think we know what will be around the bend, but there, quite unexpected, freshly white and waxen, newly pushed up through the brown leaf-mold, is a clump of Indian-pipes, erect but fragile-looking! We remember them happily from other summers and spontaneously welcome them to this year's woodland community.

Indian-pipes represent a strange group of plants—the *saprophytes*. It's a tremendous group, including many of the fungi (mushrooms among them) but actually only a few flowering plants—probably less than 20. All *saprophytes* lack chlorophyll and therefore are unable, through photosynthesis, to manufacture their own food. Instead they are dependent upon decaying organic material. Parasitic plants, also without chlorophyll, depend upon other living plants. For instance, the beechdrop, takes its nourishment from the roots of a beech tree. Another parasitic flowering plant, commonly recognized is dodder. Some appeared, uninvited, in a pot of nasturtiums we had planted!

In the case of the Indian-pipe, the decaying humus in deep wood, supplies the organic material required. There must be a significant accumulation of humus. Fallen trees, twigs and leaves must first have fallen and have been largely decomposed by beetles, ants, and other insects and by a succession of various fungi. Then the mosses and *saprophytes* can move in and do their part in converting the forest floor into a rich, fertile seedbed for the higher plants.

The Indian-pipe, with its white stalk, white scale-like leaves, and white flower, sometimes tinged with pink, is lovely and appears unreal. Sometimes it's called "corpse-plant" which is easy to understand because it grows like an apparition, a phantom flower as it stands perhaps 6 inches tall against the brown leaf-mold. It's also called "ice-plant", and indeed, when it catches a ray of sunlight it appears to be icy. One solitary flower nods from the tip of each stalk, suggesting, when it is fresh, the bowl of a pipe. Once fertilized, probably by small insects, it no longer nods but is held upright, the seed-capsule taking on the form of a small, narrow-necked brown jug. This assures the gradual dispersal of the minute seeds throughout the winter, during which the plant, then stiff and black, persists. If you should pick it now it will turn black immediately. Furthermore, it is next to impossible to transplant—as are all *saprophytes*.

There is always interesting lore associated with unusual plants. Often these tales are based on valid facts. Indeed, many of today's medicines include chemicals synthesized from plants which our American Indians used for treatment of their ills. Indian-pipes have their share of this lore.

In Mrs. William Starr Dana's book *How to Know the Wild Flowers*, (published in 1893), she states, of the Indian-pipe: "it was used by the Indians as an eye lotion, and is still believed by some to possess healing properties."

Substantiating this claim is an entry in *A Guide to the Medicinal Plants of the United States*, by Arnold and Connie Krochmal, published in 1973: "The dried powdered root was given to children for epilepsy and convulsions. Indians mixed the juice of the pulverized plant with water and used it as an eye lotion. At one time the dried plant was used in place of opium to relieve pain and induce sleep. Settlers used the fresh juice for a wide range of eye ailments."

Legend or fact, I know that if I had been city-bound and

then had the good fortune to walk on a woodland trail and gaze down on a clump of lovely, white Indian-pipes, I would find the sight "good for sore eyes".

Aug. 15, 1996

GREAT CRESTED FLYCATCHER

One morning in late May we noticed a basically gray bird, a bit smaller than a robin, investigating a birdhouse within easy sight of our big window. As it clung to the entrance-hole (which had been enlarged by red squirrels) its long, rufous tail identified it as a great crested flycatcher. The bird then entered the house but soon left—and, so far as we know, never returned to it.

The bird was probably a male, newly arrived from the southland (Mexico or northern South America). He'd have been exploring for possible nesting sites in suitable feeding territory. Apparently our birdhouse did not measure up to his standards.

This largest of America's flycatchers is the only member of its family to use birdhouses. Given its choice, the great-crested flycatcher will almost invariably select a mature hardwood woodland. There, in some tree cavity, a former woodpecker's nest or perhaps a hole caused by storm or disease, the male and female flycatchers, working together, will construct their nest. Nowadays there aren't enough suitable tree cavities to serve the birds who need them. Most of the holenesters have adapted to changed conditions, even to the point of accepting man-placed birdhouses for raising their broods. The great-crested flycatcher is one such species. The largest of America's flycatchers, it is the only flycatcher known to use birdhouses.

They're not terribly fussy about dimensions. The only absolute requirements are that the entrance hole be large enough that the adults can enter the cavity which in turn must be spacious enough to accommodate a rather bulky nest for up to six lively nestlings. Ideally, the box will have inside measurements of 6 x 6 x 10 inches, its entrance hole will be 8 inches above the floor, and it will be mounted on a tree or post at a height of 8 or 10 feet above the ground. However, these birds have been found nesting 70 feet above the ground and in boxes of almost any shape, if the two basic needs are met. If a cavity is too deep they can cope with that problem by building up the interior with bulky material.

This is a bold bird. In contesting for the same territory, it will engage in aerial combat with other males. Sometimes the feathers fly! The bird is quite vigorous in defense of its nest and has been known, also, to come to the defense of a distressed smaller bird within its territory, perhaps against a common enemy. Another species in this family, the coues flycatcher of our southwest, is so fierce in its protection of its nesting territory, attacking jays, hawks, squirrels, and snakes, that smaller songbirds like to nest nearby, thus safeguarded by the flycatchers.

This large family of birds is called the tyrant flycatcher family, *tryannidae*. The Greek word *tyfannos* means "monarch" or "ruler". Of all the songbirds these species are considered the most aggressive. Within the family are several genera. The great-crested flycatcher's genetic name is *myarchus*, which translates as "flying king," and its specific name is *crinitus*, which is from the Latin word for hair, *crinus*, and refers to the crest. Eight different species of flycatchers breed in Maine; four others are seen during migration or occasionally.

Considering the aggressive audacity of the great-crested flycatchers, I believe that our birdhouse was rejected principally because it was not deep enough. It probably measures 6x7x8 inches.

Once a suitable cavity has been agreed upon, the two birds, working together, build up a base of dead leaves, twigs and leafstalks which will then support a nest fashioned from various stems and fibers, pine-needles, grass, rootlets, feathers—a piece of castoff snake skin or a strip of plastic film, apparently for sheen! It will be lined with fur or feathers or hair to provide a soft cushion for the eggs and nestlings. Onto this cushion the female will lay one egg each day until the clutch of from four to six eggs is complete.

Then, for two weeks (13-15 days) she alone will incubate the eggs. The hatchlings will be naked at first but are soon covered with down and they will spend the next two weeks as nestlings, fed devotedly by both parents.

In 1981 I was alerted by a friend that great-crested fly-catchers were nesting close to her vegetable stand. The adults were already feeding the hatchlings when I first saw the nest. With people talking and with cars coming and going, the two parents continued feedings. I saw gauzy wings, perhaps those of a damsel-fly, in the grip of a parent's beak. It seemed a dry, crisp meal for a tiny bird which, perhaps, was fed only the soft abdomen. All sorts of insects are caught— bees, wasps, various flies, mosquitoes, grasshoppers, crick-ets, moths, butterflies, caterpillars, and at least 52 kinds of beetles!

Spiders are taken and, although very few flycatchers include fruit in their diet, the great-crested flycatcher likes to enhance its intake with berries, cherries, and wild grapes! Much of the insect food is, of course, found on the leaves and trunks of deciduous trees which is why the nest-boxes placed within easy flying range of a stand of broad-leaved trees are readily accepted.

On June 29 in 1981, the flycatcher babies in the observed nest were quite active and were uttering calls quite charac-teristic of the parent's loud "Wheep!" but with less volume. On Friday, July 3, one youngster fell out of the nest and did not survive. On July 5 my friend called to report that four active babies poked their heads from the entrance-hole. The next day another nestling fell but survived the fall. The rest fledged soon after that and the parents would surely have helped them secure food until they were able to cope for themselves. We figured that the entire project spanned a period of almost six weeks!

Aug. 15, 1996

A PLACE OF WONDER

"Blue above, brown under,
All the world to me
Is a place of wonder."
— *Robert Louis Stevenson*

Our 8 year old granddaughter, Anya Heyl, returned to her home in Minnesota last Saturday after a two-week visit in Maine. For the first week, she stayed in a rented cottage on West Harbor Pond with her dad (our son, Jack) and her aunt (our daughter, Mary Liz). The fun that week was centered around the opportunities which a freshwater pond offers— swimming, canoeing, watching the wild creatures which are part of that habitat.

Anya is the child who two years ago said of herself, "I can swim underwater but not on top and I always have to come up for air." Now she can swim "on top," too! Mary Liz, a former waterfront camp counselor, helped Anya with her swimming techniques and, most afternoons, the two of them swam across the pond and back, a fine exercise. For Anya's "half birthday," which we celebrate each summer, we had had a basswood paddle made for her height with "ANYA", carved across the handle. The week included a lot of canoeing with Anya usually paddling bow. It was never fast canoeing— there were too many interesting things to see.

Turtles basked in the sun on logs where trees had fallen into the water and on rocks near the shore. These were the painted turtles (common denizens of freshwater ponds) whose principal food is plant material. They seldom attain a length of over six inches. Another water turtle must also dwell in that pond because there were very few young ducks on West Harbor Pond this summer. One new brood of mallards hatched toward the end of that week. When first seen there were seven ducklings—just little fluffs of birds. The next day there were only six. If there really is a snapper there, more baby ducks will have disappeared by now for the snapper grows to a length of 10-12 inches and can weigh up to 35 pounds. It feeds on both plants and animals and is fond of duckling for dinner!

In a small cove, if they paddled in quietly, there was usually a great-blue heron feeding. Once Anya watched a heron catch a fish and could see how the bird's neck expanded to accommodate the catch. They also saw the little green heron fly across the pond. One day they saw a solitary sandpiper feeding daintily along a stretch of sandy shore where the water was shallow. These little shorebirds would have nested in the muskeg country of Canada and are already on their southward migration, destination Georgia, Florida, perhaps as far south as southeast Argentina.

Anya noticed the pickerelweed in blue blossom in the shallow cove where the heron fished and she was truly impressed with the beauty of the rose-petaled waterlily. These closed at mid-afternoon. Before that time, she could gaze down into the blossom, see the mass of yellow stamens and, often, watch a bee work its way down to the treasure.

That week slid by all too quickly and, then the scene and the concentration of activity shifted. Our son and daughter returned to their respective homes; Anya stayed in our house for another week. What fun we had! The emphasis, that week, was on saltwater opportunities although we did spend one afternoon at the pond during which Anya swam across the lake (wearing her life-jacket) with John and I paddling within easy reach. Then we paddled around a bit, Anya on the floor of the canoe this time, so she could point out to us her favorite places—where the heron feeds, where the baby ducks swim with their mother, where large schools of tiny fish (shiners?) swim in shallow water, some of them to become heron food, of course.

I should also mention that during the first week she and her dad had driven to Pemaquid, explored the tidepools and returned with some treasurers, one of which was a teeny weeny starfish, not more than 1/2 inch in diameter. This she later dried on a stone and her Uncle Tony, a silversmith, will cast it in silver for her.

The highlight of Anya's second week was a trip to Monhegan Island. The sea was calm and the weather was beautiful. We sat on the top deck of the "Balmy Days II" and didn't miss much. However, we saw no seals or dolphins and no whale.

Once on the island we headed straight for Cathedral Woods Trail, because that's where Monhegan children have constructed little stick houses for the elves and fairies. Anya's reaction was very positive and enthusiastic. She selected a spot she thought would be enhanced by another fairy-dwelling and so she constructed it then and there. While she was thus occupied, her architect-grandfather did some essential restoration of some nearby houses which had suffered partial collapse!

We retraced then to the main trail from which we picked up the trail which leads to Black Head. Here the gulls were active— and grateful that a little girl was willing to share some of her sandwich. The trailing juniper (often called "trailing yew" on Monhegan) formed dense mats here and, nestled in rock crevices, were little pockets of pretty three-leaved cinquefoil.

Along the trail we took Anya's picture. She was perched on the same low, horizontal branch on which Jeff's picture had been snapped when he was even younger than Anya is now—six years old, perhaps. Jeff is 17 this summer and has just completed his job on the waterfront staff of his Boy Scout Camp in the Pocono Mountains of Pennsylvania. But he's flying up for a week in Maine before school starts.

Anya and her Grandpa even walked to the ice pond after Black Head. There they saw three small ducks which John thinks may have been female or juvenile green teals. Along that path the green fringed orchid bloomed.

There were other orchids, actually along the main trail from which the others branched. These were helleborine, a rare alien orchid, carefully marked, and the small purple-fringed orchid which chooses wet places like swamps and ditches in which to bloom. It was gratifying to note that, in spite of the influx of "day-trippers," people do respond with respect to the requests of the islanders that the wild plants be left alone, allowed to live out their lives where they grow. We saw no evidence of abuse.

The trip home was calm and we were not on the top deck. That didn't matter—Anya slept most of the way back to Boothbay Harbor!

Before Anya left for the Boston Airport last Saturday she scattered extra food on our deck for her bird, chipmunk, and squirrel friends, was happy that the hummingbird had sipped from the nasturtiums that morning, and called back to the chickadee on the hanging feeder, "Goodbye! See you next year!"

Aug. 17, 1989

AUTUMN

There is something in the autumn that is
   native to my blood—
Touch of manner, hint of mood;
And my heart is like a rhyme,
With the yellow and the purple and the
   crimson keeping time.

The scarlet of the maples can shake me like a cry
Of bugles going by
And my lonely spirit thrills
To see the frosty asters like a smoke upon the hills.

—Bliss Carmen

MIGRATION MIRACLE

The southward migration of birds which bred in Maine and even farther north began several weeks ago—even in August—and it is still underway in October. When we walked at Spruce Point on Sunday we saw dozens of magnolia warblers, their yellow rumps and white tailpatches obvious as they flew. A wood thrush fed from the ground outside our door.

Robert Arbib refers to bird migration as "the semi-annual miracle and of the two avian journeys, the one which occurs in autumn is, although less obvious to humans, the more astonishing feat—the greater miracle." With many species, the first individuals to undertake the southward trip are juveniles. Their destination is the same feeding-ground which their parents left last spring. How do they know where to go?

Oh, the ornithologists have scientific terms for the miracle—"migratory instinct", "magnetic sense", "inherited faculty". Technical equipment plus the accumulation of the recorded observations of scientists and amateurs around the world enable us, today, to know a great deal about this phenomenon. Recent studies indicate that day-fliers use the sun for orientation and that night-fliers depend upon stars. It's a complex subject and many facets of migration remain a mystery.

It is estimated that more than 90 percent of the bird species which breed in northern United States, Canada, and the arctic migrate to some degree. Some of the migrants make fantastically long journeys (as from Alaska to Argentina and from the arctic to the Antarctic); others travel no more than a few hundred miles. Some species fly during the night, others are day-fliers.

Most of the small songbirds, being dayfeeders, fly during the night. Let's focus our attention on one of these: the magnolia warbler. It nests in Maine, preferring evergreen or mixed

deciduous—evergreen woodland, but the birds we watched on Sunday might have nested in Nova Scotia or New Brunswick or as far north and east as Newfoundland. Perhaps they had spent all of Saturday's clear night in the sky—or perhaps Sunday was their second or third day in this area. When they arrive at dawn, they're tired and hungry. By this time, the owl and the raccoon are well fed and are ready for sleep. Neighborhood cats may still be on the prowl but, after a night of mousing, they are not quite the menace they'd have been when the night was young. True, the insatiable weasel and some of the day-flying hawks are threats to their safety but, alternately resting and feeding, the warblers, vireos, wrens, thrushes, flycatchers, and other small night-migrants will succeed in replacing the body fat they had burned up during the night's flight. Few of them come of the feeder; they rely on wild food, most of it insects.

The magnolia warblers checked out the food supply in small spruce and pine trees, bayberry, and winterberry shrubs. One obligingly searched the grass below us as we stood looking down to the sea. Nowhere near as vividly plumaged as it would have been last spring, that bird had a soft, warm-toned back, muted stripes on its flanks, pale wingbars, and just the suggestion of an eye-ring. It did not spread its tail, revealing the white patches, until it flew. Perhaps it took off at sundown, resuming its flight toward Mexico, some other Central American country, or perhaps a Caribbean Island.

For most songbirds, 200 miles is a normal one-night lap in the long journey which, depending upon the species and also the traveling conditions, may take up to several weeks. The autumn migration is usually more leisurely than the northward one in spring probably because there is not the urgency to breed. The tiny ruby-throated hummingbird is an exception to the short-lap rule. It flies low over the white-caps, crossing the Gulf of Mexico non-stop. That distance is 600 miles!

Among the greatest hazards to the night fliers are storms, especially over water, and skyscrapers. Lighted for aircraft safety, these tall buildings often seem to lure whole flocks of tiny warblers who then crash against the concrete to their death.

Almost two thirds of North America's forest birds spend the winter in Central America, the West Indies or in the northern countries of South America, particularly Colombia, and Venezuela. The concentration of birds in those areas will be much denser than here. Most species will have less than half the territory they claimed in North America but since they have only themselves to feed (no clamoring nestlings) they can manage. The vegetation is very different and so the insect life is different also. There are different predators and more of them. But the greatest threat to many of them is that the winter range is an area that has one of the world's greatest population explosions. Everywhere, forests are falling to make room for farms.

So, fare-thee-well, you night-fliers and you day-fliers. We hope for your safe return to Maine next spring!

Oct. 20, 1983

FROM LITTLE ACORNS GROW

Nineteen ninety-three has produced a bumper crop of acorns. The upper boughs of our tall red oak trees, heavy with these fruits, lean toward the ground. Some acorns have already fallen, having been dislodged by squirrels and/or wind. Today we'll focus on the oak tree's fruit: the acorn—its uses by man and wildlife and its niche in the forest community.

The most important distinction among oak trees is between those whose acorns mature in one year and those whose acorns require two years for development. All of those in the first group are considered white oaks. Their leaves have rounded lobes. The other group is known as the black oak or the red oak group, depending on the authority, and their leaves have sharp-tipped lobes.

I know of two large white oak trees in mid-coastal Maine. One is on a road out of Nobleboro and another is on Route 27, near the Dresden-Wiscasset Town Line. They are both handsome specimens of *quercus alba*. Recently while walking the trails at Dodge Point, Newcastle, we have noticed a few white oak saplings. These may have been purposely planted by former owners—or did animals carry the acorns in?

Red oak is the most common of all Maine's oak trees. Our species is northern red oak. There's a particularly lovely red oak tree on Cross Point Road in Edgecomb. It's a really big tree and a beautiful example of how this tree develops when planted in the open. These particular trees won't win any national citations, but they must be among the largest in Maine and most of these are found only in our southern counties. There are a few red oak trees along the West Branch of the Penobscot River.

Indians depended upon acorns as a staple item in their diet. They even boiled out the tannic acid of the bitter red oak acorns and then ground them into meal. John Jossely wrote of the oil of the white oak acorns, "The Indians used this oil to anoint their naked limbs...they eat it likewise with their meat. It is an excellent clear and sweet oil..."

A wide variety of wildlife depends heavily upon the annual crop of acorns for sustenance. They relish both the sweeter white nutmeats of the white oak's and the bitter yellow meats of the red oak's acorns. Among the wild creatures nourished by acorns are many songbirds, game birds, deer, foxes, raccoon, opossum, gray and red squirrels, chipmunks, mice, and other small rodents. The acorn is well chosen by these wild creatures. It contains valuable nutrients including carbohydrates, fats, and vitamins.

A "bumper crop" of acorns occurs about every three or four years. A healthy, prolific tree may produce as many as 75,000 acorns, while the average crop, per mature oak tree is more like 5,000 acorns. It is estimated that only about one percent of those that fall to the ground sprout and of these half do not survive the seedling state. What happens to the other 99 percent?

Most of the solid ones, as we have stated, are eaten by birds and mammals. White oak acorns, being more palatable, are the first in demand; hence a smaller proportion of them are left to germinate. But the mammals do not relish the decaying acorns and these play an important role in the complex life of the forest. Moths, wasps, and other insects may have laid their eggs on the surface of the acorn while it still clung to the tree; acorn weevils and some beetles bore into acorns to lay their eggs. Other larvae and fungi may have attacked them before falling to the ground. Even if intact when they drop, they may soon be utilized for food or shelter by snails, ants, centipedes, and some creatures too small for the naked eye to observe. As the larvae hatch, as they eat their way out, they create tunnels in the nutmeat and in the shell. Gradually the acorn crumbles and is eventually recycled into humus, by decay bacteria, earthworms, and other tiny members of the forest community.

Wildlife benefits from more than the acorns. The trees provide cover for various species. The leaves of the white oak tree which have clung to the twigs throughout most of the winter are used as nesting material by many species of birds.

The little *Golden Nature Guide* for trees is excellent for identification. All of the text is accurate without being too scientific; the illustrations by Dorothea and Sy Barlowe are great. Especially fine are the pages picturing acorns. Every child and adult should have this guide. My battered copy was purchased in 1956 and, then, the price for a paperback edition was $1.25!

Sept. 30, 1993

GEORGE'S ISLAND

A little more than a week ago (Tues., Oct. 21, 1980), on a beautiful, sunny afternoon, John and I launched our little yellow canoe at West Harbor Pond. We paddled the circumference of this lovely lake, admiring the bright colors of the trees along the shore. At "George's Island" we beached the canoe and walked over its paths and noted its vegetation.

Our grandson, Jeff, loves this island and when, last summer, he, his mother and another young boy canoed on the pond they always beached here. Twice they cooked their lunch and even brought home litter left by other campers.

Do you wonder why we call this place "George's Island"? Jeff loves the story. He quite identifies with George.

One day when we spoke of canoeing on West Harbor Pond, a friend of ours, George, told us why he always thinks of that little island as his own.

George's grandmother lived long enough to be important in George's memory. When he was a young boy, she lived in a small frame house on the side of a hill near but not on the shore of West Harbor Pond. She also owned "Little Marsh Island".

When George was old enough (about 12 or 14 years, he thinks) one of his chores was to go to the woodlot to prepare fuel for the kitchen stove. He brought his axe and he carried a jug of coffee. Sometimes he'd bring a friend with him and when the job was done, the boys walked across the ice to Little Marsh Island. George writes: "The greatest delight on the island was spruce gum which all the boys and men chewed."

I had pictured George exploring the island in the summertime, reaching it by rowboat, canoe, raft, or even by swimming to it. And I thought that he and his friends had probably pitched a tent there and cooked a good bacon and smoked-egg breakfast. But, no, his only access to the island was by foot in the wintertime. But he loved Little Marsh

Island. (This island is not at all marshy, nor is it surrounded by marsh. We suppose it received that name long before there was a West Harbor Pond. "Campbell's Cove" had been an arm of the sea before it was dammed in 1879 to create a freshwater pond for ice-harvesting.)

George often "sat" for his grandmother when she could no longer be left alone and later, when she lived at his parents' home, he must have been helpful to her in many ways. One day the conversation went something like this:

"George, you're so good to me. I'd like to give you something or do something for you—to say thank you. What would you like?"

"Oh, Gran, you know I don't want anything!"

"George, I don't mean money. There must be something of mine you'd like to have for your very own. Come now, isn't there?"

I wonder if his grandmother knew what George would ask for. The youth must have stammered a bit but then encouraged by her, he blurted out, "Well, Gran, if you really what to know— there's only one thing you own that I would really love to have. It's—the island!"

"Good! George, it's yours. I give it to you today and as soon as I can see a lawyer I'll make it a legal gift."

But Mary died before she could legalize the gift and Little Marsh Island was sold as part of her estate. I don't know who owns it today and I don't believe George does either.

But does it matter? It's still there in the pond, its trees dropping fruits and leaves to make an ever-deeper woodsloam. Today the dominant trees are red oak, white pine, red and white spruce. There are also large-toothed aspen, gray and white birches, choke-cherry, and there's a lot of balsam and juniper. Beneath these there are bayberry and sweet gale, steeplebush, blueberries, and wild rose. There were asters and goldenrod in bloom there last week and hugging the ground were mosses, lichens, and many mushrooms.

We saw robins, juncos, and myrtle warblers and there must be many other birds who scout there successfully for seeds and fruits and insects. It's a healthy, very lovely little island—and, fortunately it's too small for a home. The chances are good that it will be there, very much as it is now, for a long time.

So you see why we call this place "George's Island" which, in George's heart it will always be.

"So let me keep these treasures of the humble heart
In true possession owning them by love."
                                            - Henry Van Dyke

Oct. 30, 1980

HALLOWEEN HOOTERS

Halloween is certainly an appropriate time for a wildlife column to feature owls. Although their hoots and calls and screams may pierce the air they are rarely seen by human beings. Their images, nevertheless, are familiar to all of us; the black silhouette of an owl, cut by a child from black paper, appears on many a window at this time of year. It is as much a symbol of Halloween as is the pumpkin or a witch.

Maine has very large owls and owls that are quite small. We have six permanent resident species and four which breed farther north but sometimes wander into our area in wintertime. In the first group, those that breed here in Maine and may be seen or heard in all months of the year, are, (the smallest to largest) the saw-whet, screech, short-eared, long-eared, barred, and great-horned owls. The winter visitors are the boreal, hawk, snowy, and great gray owls.

Each species of owl has its own distinctive call—sometimes quite loud and "scary"—and they all have silent flight, both of which features contribute to the awe with which they are regarded.

The tiny saw-whet owl has a rasping call responsible for its common name. But the screech owl, not very much bigger, is ineptly named. It resembles a European owl in appearance and that owl does, indeed, screech, but our species' call has been described as "the most plaintively sweet and doleful of all bird utterances...suggestive of the prolonged, subdued whinny of a small horse."

The short-eared owl, a bird of the open countryside, is not a very vocal creature. But if, in the springtime, you hear, probably in the afternoon, a long series of up to 20 hoots or toots, you just might be hearing the courtship call of a male short-eared owl. These owls also have a cat-like call.

Unlike its short-eared cousin, which often hunts by day, the long-eared owl is strictly nocturnal. It has quite a variety of calls, including a cat-like snarl. During the March mating season the male's courtship call is a soft, deep "hoo-ood, hoo-ood."

Now we come to the big fellows. The barred owl, with a body length of up to 24 inches and a wingspread of up to 50 inches, is actually quite numerous throughout its range, which includes the entire eastern part of the Untied States. But were it not for the jays and crows who create quite a commotion when they discover a barred owl trying to rest amid dense evergreen foliage, we'd never know that the barred owl is a member of our wildlife community—unless at night we hear his 8-hooted call "Who-who-who-who, Who cooks for you-all" (the last note is lured downward) or, much worse, his terrifying shriek. I've heard that shriek only once and I'll never forget it, although I'll undoubtedly be just as stunned if I ever hear it again. We were coming out of the woods, at dusk, very weary after a long and difficult hike to Green Falls in Baxter Park, when shrieks which sounded as though a woman were being attacked, rent the

September air. You stood still and trembled—but our more knowledgeable companions, Miriam Schantz and Harold Colt, laughed after the first jolt and reassured us. "That's only a barred owl." This owl is said to be uncommon along the coast—but Edgecomb is not very far inland and our friends along Mill Road in that town often hear "the eight-hooter."

The great-horned owl is even a bit bigger than the barred. The female may be as long as 25 inches and its wing-spread reaches 6 inches. The male is somewhat smaller. This is the fellow who is often called "the hoot owl". His resounding hoot has a less regular pattern than that of the barred owl.

The utterances of the owls which visit us irregularly in the wintertime follow the general pattern that large owls have deep voices, small owls have highly pitched calls. The little boreal owl has a repetitive "ting-ting-ting". The hawk owl's call has been likened to that of the osprey and also to that of the kestrel. But both the snowy and the great gray owls have deep resonant hoots. It is claimed that the deep booming of the snowy owl can carry at least seven miles!

All of these calls, whether of high or low pitch, are for communication between individuals of the same species. Although we might not distinguish between the call of a male and a female barred owl, the barred owls definitely do recognize the difference! The calls are used by both sexes to declare hunting territory—and by the cock to attract females. "Their hoots and screams make up a well developed language." (John Sparks and Tony Soper, in *Owls, Their Natural and Unnatural History*.)

Owls seem to be most vocal in autumn and spring and, of course, the cock's calls to attract females precede the nesting season. The large owls nest very early—even late January—so their hoots are most evident in autumn and early winter.

The chances are that if on Halloween night you hear a series of weird booming hoots, they come not from a ghost or goblin but from a great horned owl.

Oct. 29, 1981

A SNUFF OF SKUNK

For the past week or so the grass around our house has been pocked with holes, some of them as deep as my longest finger, none wilder than its depth. Each morning there are a few new holes. In some cases the sod, as if a carpet, is rolled to one side. I can roll it back into place, covering the cavity.

These holes are made by skunks; yet seldom have we been aware of the odor associated with this mammal. If a dog should roam at large at night, however, he'd be likely to notice this hungry prowler and if the dog were too assertive, the skunk would use his defense weapon. We'd know of the encounter; so would the neighbors, and the owners of the dog might resort to giving their pet alternative baths of tomato juice and vinegar-water—outdoors!

The fluid sprayed from the anal glands of the skunk is potent, indeed, and it is persistent. "I have no doubt the essence of the skunk has some rare medicinal properties, if one has the courage to use it," wrote John Burroughs to a friend (c. 1890). In an amusing anecdote John James Audubon's friend, The Rev. John Bachman, tells of a clergyman for whose distressing asthma his doctor prescribed the snuffing of shunk musk. Rev. Bachman procured the glands of a skunk for his friend. They were kept "Tightly corked in a snuff-bottle" to be applied to the nose when necessary. It was an effective remedy but once he uncorked his bottle during a sermon—"His congregation—made a hasty retreat, leaving him alone in the church..."

What should be our attitude toward this wild creature who shares these open-wooded acres with us? Let's consider the question selfishly. Are the skunks beneficial to the human residents of this neighborhood or would we be better off without them? Almost every general article on skunks mentions the holes made in grass during the autumn and states that the purpose of the digging, accomplished with the pointed nose, is to secure insect larvae, especially beetle grubs. People with close-cropped, well-groomed lawns become annoyed and often call their local police departments, requesting assistance in ridding the area of the offenders. But which is worse—to have skunks or beetle grubs? To find the answer sent me to the insect books.

The skunks prize find is the larva of the junebug or june beetle, which is the large insect which buzzes around lights on early summer evenings. The female deposits her eggs in earth surrounded by grass roots. White grubs hatch from these eggs and they grow to be about the size of a man's small finger. They may stay in the larval stage for two or three years and they feed upon grass roots. Uncontrolled these grubs can ruin a lawn. When they become adults they "feed on flowers and foliage of various trees and shrubs and are capable of completely defoliating them." (*A Field Guide to the Insects* by Donald J. Boritor and Richard E. White.)

Here we have an example of the balance of nature and also of food-chains. In claiming part of this neighborhood for our own habitat we opened up the woodland enough to encourage the growth of grass—which in turn offered hospitality to female junebugs searching for a suitable place to lay eggs. The grubs, hatched from the eggs and other grass-feeding insects, meadow voles, etc. attract the skunk. The great horned owl finds the combination of tall pine trees, prowling skunks and rodents a satisfactory nesting and

hunting area. These are all native American species. They keep each other in check. The owls, at the top of the food-chain, will be controlled by the food supply; when that is not ample they will move away or they will have smaller broods. There may be a cyclical peak of junebugs one year, a responding peak of skunks the next, and the owls will be abundant the following year. Will you go along with me and allow the skunk its niche in our complex wildlife community?

We should know more about this wild neighbor than that its defense weapon is a gummy, malodorous fluid and that it eats grubs, salamanders, small rodents, etc.

The home is a burrow in the ground or under a boulder or a rock—or wood-pile or even beneath an abandoned building. In our part of the country, there is only one litter. Mating season is late winter and the young (from two to ten, usually four to six) are born in May after a gestation period of 62 to 64 days. The babies are blind, deaf, and nearly naked at birth but the thin coat of hair already shows the black-and-white fur pattern. By the time they are three weeks old, they'll be fully furred and the eyes will have opened but they'll nurse until they're two months old.

By this time of year the parents and the young are fatten-ing up for the cold months ahead, during which they are often dormant but not truly hibernating. The males tend to be solitary during the winter but several females and their young may den together. A January thaw may lure them, especially the males, out of their retreats to search for fresh food. The great horned owl hopes so; one skunk may be his dinner that warm night.

Frank Gramlich, Maine's director of the U.S. Bureau of Wildlife Assistance at Augusta, feels strongly that skunks "earn their right to life in human neighborhoods." He says, "To me a skunk is an aesthetic thing. I like to see a skunk bumping along my lawn at night."

Oct. 23, 1980

BRIGHT RED BERRIES

Many kinds of bright red berries are being harvested by birds and mammals of the wildlife community. If we walk in the woods or along their edges we can see the berries; in most cases we do not see the harvesters. But if we check the same places, at one-week intervals, we know that much has already been eaten or toted away to be hoarded. And we are given clues as to which species are most popular.

I checked a spot on our own property where there had been a heavy crop of partridgeberries. These are the fruits of the ground-creeping plant which has small, heart-shaped, paired, evergreen leaves. It is a favorite for inclusion in terrariums. I had to really search to find just four red berries; perhaps a partridge (ruffed grouse) had dined there. Mockingbirds, quail, raccoons, red fox, skunk, and wood mice also eat the partridgeberry. This patch is close to the barberry shrubs where a late flock of robins feasted last week. The birds on the ground may have been eating partridgeberries. But in other years we have found patches of partridgeberry still laden with red fruit in December. When there's a light snow on the forest floor and tiny, wind-blown seeds are hidden, the red berries gleaming pink through the snow must be a welcome sight for a hungry woodland denizen.

Another red berry which, if not harvested before deep snow comes, will be even more delicious after having been frozen all winter is wintergreen, or teaberry. Pheasant and even black bear will nibble on these—so will humans. They have a refreshing taste due to the aromatic oil characteristic of this plant and also of the black and the yellow birches.

We also have bunchberry or ground dogwood near our home. Earlier this autumn hundreds of clusters of bright red, opaque fruits, almost the size of blueberries, gleamed among the plant's own typically dogwood-veined leaves and hairy-cap moss. Then it was clear that what in springtime had appeared to be single flowers with four white petals were, instead, clusters of many flowers, framed by four white bracts. There are many species of dogwood, some of them trees, some tall shrubs, and the fruits of all of them, whether red or white or blue, provide important food for wildlife.

In our area, bunchberry is the most common dogwood. Many birds, including all of the thrushes, are happy to find bunchberries where they pause to rest and feed on their southward journeys. What they leave, the squirrels and mice will find. When I looked today I knew that some feasting had occurred!

There are many other red, berry-like fruits which provide food for wildlife. There is bittersweet, so popular for decorative purposes and also enjoyed as food by squirrels, gamebirds, and many songbirds. There are the sumacs, their fruits held high above the snow. These are not favorite wildlife fare, but when the going is tough they serve as survival food. There's mountain ash. Our native tree is red-fruited; the European species has orange fruit. There's highbush cranberry, which is really not a cranberry but a *viburnum*, *viburnum trilobum*.

I think my favorite red-berried plant is winterberry. We like to walk along the ocean between Grimes Cove and the Ocean Point Inn and we do so in all seasons. But we can pass by the winterberry without noticing it except in mid and late autumn. Its small, greenish white flowers were inconspicuous in late spring; later the slowly ripening, berry-like drupes were hidden by abundant green leaves. No feature of the plant demands our attention. But when the flame on the hardwood trees subsides and the shrub's own leaves become sparse, these lovely red fruits are revealed, ripe and bright.

It's really a holly—*Ilex verticillate*; yet more people, at least here in New England, refer to it as black alder. "Yon alder's crimson beads" is the way John G. Whittier referred to these clusters. James Russell Lowell put it this way, "With coral beads, the prim black alders shine." But, botanically this shrub is a holly—a deciduous holly. I like to use its other common name, winterberry, although it is true that in our northern states the fruits which are not harvested by wildlife for food or by humans for decoration will drop by midwinter.

Although Harriet Keeler in *Our Northern Shrubs* remarks, "The birds, it seems, will have none of them, the thin flesh is too nauseous and the nutlets are too many..." my own observations are to the contrary and other sources state that this fruit is a choice food of the mockingbird and that several species of song and game birds relish it. So do small rodents. Thoreau wrote on Nov. 19, 1857 of the wood mouse and this plant: "What pretty fruit for them these bright berries! They run up the twigs in the night and gather this shining fruit, take out the small seeds and eat these kernels at the entrance to their burrows. The ground is strewn with them."

One year, in early November, three of us stood admiring a winterberry shrub along the seaward side of Ocean Point Road. The plant was about twice our height and scarlet with fruits. This was late afternoon; the berries glowed in the light of the setting sun; it was a lovely sight. Then we noticed motion among the twigs. A female pine grosbeak, new to us then, was feeding on the berries. She accommodated us by changing positions as she continued to feast, almost as if to display her various features. That was an incident we'll never forget.

Nov. 17, 1983

DRUM ROLL

"Ruffed grouse"—to some people those words suggest a delicious meal of wildfowl, prepared for the table after an exhilarating day in the woods with gun and dog. Others recall times they've sneaked up quietly on the bird to spy on him during his courtship act. They've seen him spread his ruff and strut; they've seen him on his "drumming-log" and they've heard him drum. Our friend, Miriam Schantz, of Emmaus, Pa., is one of these.

Miriam, who works as a bookkeeper for Bethlehem Steel Company, spends as much of her free time as possible out-of-doors. She introduced us to Baxter Park. Last May she brought a friend with her to Kidney Pond Camps who had shown interest in Miriam's outdoor pursuits.

Let me quote from Miriam's journal the passages that refer to the ruffed grouse.

"Sun., May 17, 1981: walked with Tess to Foster Field and we saw a grouse in the bushes eating the buds. Heard another one drumming in the woods and we found him on the drumming-log and he walked off! Will check the log another day." John and I were with them for part of that week. It was a joy to realize Tess' delight in this new experience. She was fascinated, especially with the grouse. Every opportunity she had she silently checked that log. After John and I had returned home, Miriam made this entry: "Thurs., May 28: Jerry and I joined Tess in the woods close to the grouse on the log. She had already seen him drum once. With some black flies tormenting us, we stood almost motionless as we saw and heard the grouse go through his spring drumming act on his mossy log. It's always a great woodsy show and we saw him do his very special thing four times (five times, for Tess). The last time was his best. He seemed to put every bit of strength into his whole body, from his erect head and sharp eyes to his powerful, fast-beating wings. His big, broad, beautiful tail which was usually quite flat on the log was up high and the ends curled up. A great performance. We walked slowly and quietly out of the woods, beaming from ear to ear. A little wild creature of the woods had turned us on. What a thrill, a joy, a privilege to be so close to this wild bundle of feathers with so much pep, vim and vigor. It was a bonus morning. We had stood at the right spot and for a few minutes the grouse had captivated us."

The sound of the ruffed grouse's booming drum-roll can be heard a quarter of a mile away. Although "the really intensive drumming is in early spring, ruffed grouse have been known to drum every month of the year, and during every hour of the day or night. There is a short period, however, in mid-autumn when drumming increases for a few weeks..." (Edminster, quoted in *Encyclopedia of North American Birds* by John K. Terres).

But few people have the opportunity to hear and see those mid-autumn performances. The woods are unsafe for silent observers, during the hunting seasons. However, no hunting is permitted in Baxter Park. Here are two autumn entries in Miriam Schantz's journal.

"Fri., Sept. 18, 1981: At Foster Field I went into the woods where in spring Tess and I saw a grouse drumming. I had a pleasant shock, as there on the log was the grouse, just as we had left him in May. I stayed and didn't move and he started his drumming act. Then he did it a second and a third time. With the sixth he beat the record we saw in May. Well, he got up to 10, to 14, and after the 16th he proudly walked the full length of the mossy log and disappeared into the woods. I stood there quietly for about three-quarters of an hour watching the grouse. One foot was asleep and I was glad to move again and happily walked out of the woods. Mr. Grouse must have had a good summer; he seemed so much bigger and fatter than in May. He was King of the Forest and I was lucky to be there. This game bird of the deep woods is so illusive to the hunter and I had him in full view 20 steps from his log. I could see every feather shake as he went through his ritual 16 times.

Thurs., Oct. 1: I stopped at Foster Field for the last check-up on the grouse. Walked quietly into the woods and there he was, standing on the log. I waited a few minutes; he looked up, stood up nice and straight, put his wing tips down and I thought he was going to drum. Instead, I was going to see something very, very special. He slowly got into his display. What a beautiful sight! First he put his tail straight up and into a big broad fan and he slowly puffed up his ruff as if blowing up a balloon. The ruff gradually got bigger and thicker and higher and it surrounded his head. He looked great. Soon I saw the female walk close to the log and that's why he was in full display. He looked like a little turkey with that perfect fan tail. He walked lengthwise several times on the log and he thought he was hot stuff. Then he stepped off the log, started to move his head and ruff from side to side, and to make little noises. Then he tried to follow the hen. She tried to avoid him and walked under the brush or flew on top of some blowdowns. All these places made it hard for the fancy cock to walk. He took great care in walking slowly through the brush to turn his big fan tail and not have it rub against the branches or twigs. I followed them through the woods. They went out on the open grass of Foster Field and no photographer was with me! She walked under the bench and picnic table and under the low bushes at the edge of the woods. He just could not get to her. After a while I lost them in the thick woods. What a lucky experience to see this tricky hen and the fancy cock trying to get to her, while shaking his big high ruff and "talking" all the time. This lovely pair of ruffed grouse gave me a real woodsy send-off. Perfect. Hope to see him again in May—on his log.

Oct. 22, 1981

HACKMATACK

We may pass by the hackmatack tree for forty-eight weeks of the year without noticing it—but in late October and early November it commands our admiring attention. After the flaming color of the hardwood trees has departed the hackmatack's lacy, needle-form leaves gleam against the autumn sky. By the time most of the red oak leaves, now a ruddy brown, have dropped and while some thin, silvery-toned beech leaves still cling to twigs, the hackmatack needles will have slowly deepened from pale yellow to a deep tawny gold. It offers a dramatic contrast to the bare deciduous trees and to the clean green of the pines, spruces, and balsams which have now recovered from the shaggy appearance they had as they shed their two-year old needles.

This tree is properly known as the American larch, *larix laricina*, and it is often referred to as tamarack—but in New England, certainly in Maine, it is generally known by its aboriginal name, hackmatack—so that's what I use.

Among New England's coniferous trees it is unique—for it, alone, sheds all of its needles each fall. Being a deciduous conifer enables the hackmatack to cope with severe weather in the far northland. It can survive farther north than any other tree in North America. Its range extends up into areas where NO transpiration or photosynthesis can occur except in the long days of the arctic summer. Therefore the hackmatack, in its adaptation to that environment, sheds all of its needles at the end of its growing period. Thus it employs two devices. Like the evergreen coniferous trees, it has slim waxy-coated needles needed for conservation of water during the growing season. And, like the broad-leaved deciduous trees, it has bare branches for a winter so cold that no water is available for transpiration. Hackmatack, as a deciduous conifer, is a brave species, a pioneer, daring to explore new territory, determined to survive. In Maine the best stands of tamarack are found north of Bangor; in fact, they seem happiest the nearer they get to the treeline of the arctic. Nevertheless, there are beautiful tamaracks in Lincoln County. Route 27 in Edgecomb and the River Road to Damariscotta have clumps of this tree, now quite golden. On Saturday we drove to Camden, up Mount Battie and also inland along Route One. We saw many tamaracks as we drove along.

A European larch, *larix decidua*, has slightly longer needles and cones and has been introduced in our country as an ornamental tree, a graceful addition to lawns and parks. It escapes into the wild by means of its wind-borne seeds. It is present as an escape tree in our own Lincoln County. But America's native larch, *larix laricina* is common in all of Maine's sixteen counties. Its first choice is a cold peat bog. In this wet and acid situation it achieves its finest potential, commonly to 80 feet in height. I do not know if it survives today, but in 1979 the largest American larch known to be living in the world grew in Jay, Maine. Its height then was 95 feet, its circumference at breast height was nine feet, eight inches, and its crown spread was 50 feet.

For the first 40 years or so of its life, a tamarack is a fast-growing tree. Then its rate of growth slows, its very resinous wood becoming hard, heavy, strong, and very durable. These characteristics make it an ideal material for several specific needs. The early boat builders used larch for "ship's knees". They dug out the stump, using the angle between the trunk and the root for this purpose. There is a record of one man digging out 378 "knees" in one winter (1849-50)—all from tamarack trees. In *Tall Trees, Tough Men* Robert W. Pike writes, "And tamarack will never rot." Thus it was sought for pins in dams and for pumps, pump-logs, and even (in one Maine village) for water mains. In our own era, it is used for planking, ties, and vats, piling, as well as for pulp. There are tales of iron cookstoves, stoked with hackmatack wood, that warped from excessive heat!

Does this larch tree have enemies? It is vulnerable to fire, especially in bogs where the burning peat kills the roots.

Its shallow root system makes it an easy victim of wind storms. There is an insect, the larch sawfly, which cyclically defoliates the hackmatack after which the weakened trees are subject to attack by bark beetles. And since porcupines enjoy the bark of the upper trunk, they sometimes cause deformation. Still, the tree's chances of achieving a healthy maturity are good.

If you have a mucky place on your property where the larch seed or young transplant can have wet roots, and sun on its leaves, you will probably soon have a beautiful young hackmatack tree. We are told that transplanting is successful only if it is done while the tree is dormant.

Indians taught the American colonists that "The turpentine that issueth from the larch tree is singularly good to heal wounds, and to drawn out the malice." (John Josselyn) and Donald Culross Peattie concludes his essay on this tree with the statement, "As long as woodsmen know their woods, the tamarack can prove their friend in time of need, for its curative powers are genuine."

There are a couple of weeks still ahead to notice this unusual tree. Its tawny spires will be especially striking just after most of the other leaves have fallen. Then their leaves, too, will drop and the trees will appear stark and bare in the winter.

Nov. 2, 1989

OF MOOSE AND MEN

This autumn's legal moose hunt (1996) closed with 1,327 of Maine's biggest mammals reported as shot. We know that there are far too many car-moose encounters, and we know that the expanding moose population can benefit by culling—but—

Those of us who have shared Maine's trails with this animal and who have watched it swim in Maine's ponds and laughed to see a bull moose raise its head from a pond's mucky bottom, its antlers dripping with cow-lily stems while it munches on a prized rhizome, fail to see how any sport is involved in killing one. We are not comfortable about the moose season.

Let's consider how the moose has fared in the more than 300 years since, in 1634, William Wood wrote in his *New England's Prospect*: "The beast called a moose is not much unlike our red deer. This beast is as big as an ox, slow of foot, head like a buck, with a broad beam, some being two yards in the head. Their flesh is as good as beef, their hides good for clothing. The English have some thoughts of keeping them tame and to accustom them to the yoke, which will be a great commodity: first, because they are so fruitful, bringing forth three at a time, being likewise very uberous ("abounding in milk", a definition from my English dictionary!); secondly, because they will live in winter without fodder…These poor beasts likewise are much devoured by wolves."

William Wood's account of early New England has been judged one of the few early accounts of the New World which emphasize natural history. It also provides insight, humor, and a feeling for conservation.

Later in the 17th-century John Josselyn, perhaps a more serious naturalist, wrote in *New England's Rarities Discovered*: "The moose-deer, which is a very goodly creature, some of them twelve foot high, with exceeding fair horns with broad palms, some of them two fathom from the tip of one horn to the other"... (a discussion of the luscious meat) and "The Indian Webbes make use of the broad teeth of the fawns to hang about their children's neck when they are breeding of their teeth."

In the early 1770s, Jacob Bailey included, in his manuscript, descriptions of some of the animals which "abound chiefly in these regions" "...First the moose, the largest and most majestic animal which grazes the American forests...He rises gradually from his underparts, advances head aloft with a noble and stately air... The ground trembles beneath his enormous weight... These remarkable animals are very common all over this country, especially on Kennebec River where great numbers are annually killed for their flesh which is tenderer than beef..."

Yet within 50 short years the moose had all but disappeared from our part of Maine. Most of the moose population, seriously depleted, had retreated to Canada.

The first closed season on moose in Maine was in 1830. We continued, however, to eradicate their

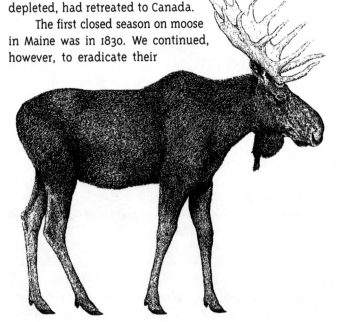

wild predators, especially the wolf. Safety from man and wolf, combined with the reversion of many stony farms to forest, thus providing browse and shelter, has resulted in a remarkable comeback in the numbers of moose in our state.

We have seen moose several times, most often in Baxter Park. Once, as six of us sat on a long log near the pebbly shore of Wassataquoil Lake, a large bull dashed past us, within five feet of me, and then proceeded to bathe in the lake. Once morning a moose came to the salt lick near Kidney Pond's lodge, crouched on his knees and then indulged his craving for salt. That was an odd picture. It was explained that a moose, because of its very long legs and short neck cannot reach down to the ground as a cow can. A moose browses but does not graze. That's why the stripped maple, which seldom attains a height of 15 feet, is called moosewood. Those mammals can reach moosewood foliage easily.

In May, 1975, with much of the forest prone and tangled following the Big Slowdown of November, 1974, the big mammals were much in evidence as they took advantage of the few trails the park men had managed to keep open. If we met a moose while hiking we moved to the side as if to say, "Pardon us,"—We felt awe but not fear. He's too big to argue with about right-of-way. A cow moose who is concerned about the safety of her calf could be dangerous, but like other browsers they are basically gentle creatures.

Our most exciting moose experience occurred just two nights before the close of our 1971 vacation at Ocean Point. We had been told, "Oh, you have to go inland to see a moose". But after enjoying a lobster dinner at Lincolnville and returning to Ocean Point via Route 1, near Warren, there suddenly was before us, broadside, a bull moose, antlers, bell, and all. We were upon him immediately. He rolled against our windshield, reducing it to sand-sized particles with which we were peppered. And, then (or neither of us could have told the tale!), he rolled off again into the ditch. John could stop the car, we were not hurt at all, and could open the car doors. But neither the moose nor the Impala survived the encounter. The game warden, after he had shot the moose, whose legs were broken, reported that the bull's 12-point rack had a 45-inch span. He estimated its live weight to have been 1,200 pounds. Later, the *Portland Press Herald* reported that the moose had dressed down at 771 pounds!

Undaunted, the very next day we signed the agreement of sale for a lot in East Boothbay—Tall wood, on which we have built our home. And that we've *never* regretted. Our drive to Allentown was in a new car!

Nov. 7, 1996

SPUNKY BUFFLEHEADS

In our part of Maine, one of November's delights is to have the loon, the grebes, and the diving ducks that winter in this area return to the coastal waters. The regal loons glide alone; "little grebies" pop about in twos and threes. There are large rafts of eiders, loose flocks of jabbering oldsquaws, smaller groups of goldeneyes, and of buffleheads. Black ducks are out there, too, and the birder with trained eye and good binoculars will notice other, less common species. So will amateurs, although we may be puzzled.

"What duck can I have seen on the Damariscotta River? It was quite big, with a lot of white on the body and it had a double crown." I showed the questioner a picture of a red-breasted merganser, with its beautiful, conspicuous crests and he agreed. "That's it!" he exclaimed. "It was the male red-breasted merganser. That's a really handsome duck!"

The birds that choose to spend the winter in and on Maine's offshore waters are rugged birds. To be sure, there's plenty of food out there and they all wear warm, well-insulated, waterproof parkas, but there are also violent storms. After these we see parts of boats, docks, lobster traps, and buoys which have succumbed to the onslaught; very seldom do we see a dead bird as a storm victim.

Today we will concentrate attention on the smallest duck, the bufflehead. I think it's my favorite. Both its scientific generic name, *bucephala*, and its nickname, bufflehead, are derived from the Greek work, *boukephalos* which translates as "ox-headed". This duck and its cousins, the goldeneyes, do have the appearance of heavy-headedness.

We usually see these spunky little ducks first on a quiet inlet. One year our earliest sighting was on a secluded part of Boothbay Harbor's West Harbor Pond. There were six males, their darkly iridescent "buffle" heads capped with bright white, their bodies sharply black and white. They were very beautiful on that calm, cattail-spiked water in the morning sun. We had to look carefully and count several times before we agreed that there were also six females. These divers are active and some in a group are always under water. I'm told, though, that they are never all under water at once; there's always at least one "on guard".

Where have they been since last April? Well, I learned that they've been far away. The buffleheads fly all the way to western Canada and into Alaska to breed. Courtship and pairing may have taken place at any resting spot along the lengthy route. In *The Birds of Brewery Creek,* Malcolm Mac-Donald tells of his fascination in observing the pairing of male and female buffleheads. Two females, the very first migrant ducks to touch down on "the creek" (near Ottawa, Canada) arrived on the first day of April. He began to consider them "spinsters"—for they loitered there a full week with no male company. On April 8th two handsome drakes flew in to Brewery Creek—but the female ducks were farther upstream. He realized that birds have almost no sense of smell—that instead they are influenced by sight and sound. He "felt a strong urge to achieve an introduction but the situation seemed hopeless." It was when a man in a boat disturbed the males that they flew in fright—to the same cove where the female buffleheads glided. The drakes were immediately "wildly excited" and wasted no time. They puffed out their head feathers and rapidly jerked their beautiful heads up and down in the courtship demonstration characteristic of this species.

At their destination they would select a tree cavity for the nest. It had probably have been carved out in some former year by a large woodpecker. The female would have added a soft lining to the cavity and would have laid in it a large clutch of eggs—up to a dozen of them. Once hatched, the precocial ducklings tumbled from the three and a quarter inch hole to the ground, their descent protected by the fluffy down on their young bodies. Their mother waited, to escort them to the water which is always nearby. There, in that northern pond mother bufflehead taught her youngsters how to dive, secure food, and how to fly. They never needed a swimming lesson!

Buffleheads seem loath to leave the northland and they often use our freshwater ponds until they are frozen over. That's why our first sighting of them is on fresh water. The buffleheads that arrive here in late October are often in family-sized groups. We welcome these little "butterballs" (that's another of their nicknames) and want to say to them, "Have a good winter!"

Nov. 17, 1994

HICKORY NUT MACAROONS

When it comes to cookies our specialty of the house is a hickory nut macaroon. The recipe was John's aunt's and so these are known as "Aunt Miriam's Hickory Nut Macaroons." They melt in your mouth; the flavor is delicious and subtle, they are easy to mix and to bake.

"Beat 3 egg whites. When foamy add 1/4 tsp. Cream of tartar. Continue beating until stiff and dry. (I suppose Aunt Miriam's arm ached but today the electric mixer whizzes through that chore.) Then fold in (gently, she says) 1 cup of sugar and 2 cups hickory nutmeats to which 1 tbsp. of flour has been added. Chill overnight or for several hours in cloth-covered bowl. Then spoon onto a well buttered cookie sheet and bake at 325 degrees until delicate brown, (about 20 minutes)." I use two large baking sheets, 30 cookies to a sheet. Be sure the oven is preheated and do not use the top element except, possibly, to lightly brown at the very end of baking time.

Isn't that simple? Yet, they are not that simple to come by.

HICKORY NUT MACAROONS

3 egg whites
1/4 tsp. cream of tarter
1 cup sugar

2 cups hickory nut meats (or pecans)
1 tbsp. flour

"Beat 3 egg whites. When foamy add 1/4 tsp. Cream of tartar. Continue beating until stiff and dry. Then gently fold in 1 cup of sugar and 2 cups hickory nutmeats to which 1 tbsp. of Flour has been added. Chill overnight or for several hours in cloth-covered bowl. Then spoon 30 cookies onto a well buttered cookie sheet and bake at 325 degrees until delicate brown, about 20 minutes.

The first challenge is to procure the nutmeats. I have shelled and picked out just enough hickory nuts to know that I'm willing to pay the $8 per pound for the nutmeats which, if I'm lucky, are found at Allentown (Pennsylvania) Farmers' Market. They are available if the trees bore well that year and also if our daughter, who lives in nearby Bethlehem, stops by the farm stand in October and orders them for pickup in November. She buys three pounds for me. That's a year's supply. They freeze well.

The second challenge is to be really sure that not a single bit of shell escaped the notice of the person who picked out the nutmeats—because the shell is very hard. One tiny fragment will ruin a cookie and perhaps a tooth. So I do a careful recheck under good light, usually the evening before I mix the ingredients.

When we lived in Allentown, I went to the Farmers' Market one Nov. day and, as I examined some hickory nutmeats through the cellophane bag, a bright-eyed, blond child, about nine years old approached me and asked, "Do you want to buy them?" "I'm checking for shells", I replied. "Oh," she told me proudly, "There aren't any shells. My grandpappy was VERY careful." She made the sale, she made the proper change (with a little help from her father) and she made me feel good as I walked away with my nutmeats, the result of a three-generation project.

It used to be, and in some farm areas it still is, the children's responsibility to gather the nuts. What could be more fun on a bright autumn day than gathering chestnuts, hickory nuts, and black walnuts with your brothers, sisters, and friends? Or taking part in a "nut crack", using hammers and stones, devouring some of the sweet nutmeats as you worked along, and saving a fine supply for the cakes, cookies, pies, and taffies of the coming winter? The nuts were the children's contribution to the Thanksgiving and Christmas feasts, and rightfully they sang with pride, "nuts are in the attic..."

In a still earlier era the Indians hoarded nuts, prizing the hickory nut especially. In *Travels in North America*

William Bartram reported that he had seen supplies of more than one hundred bushels per family among the Creeks, who boiled and crushed the nutmeats, strained the resulting brew and used this "hickory milk" as cream in corncakes and other cookery.

The delicious hickory nut is the fruit of the shagbark hickory tree, *carya ovata*. This fine forest tree is unmistakable in any season because of its distinctive bark which is smoky-gray in color and constantly curling away from the trunk in huge plates sometimes as large as 12 by 8 inches. The forest floor at the base of a large tree will be quite littered with the cast off strips.

The aromatic leaves are compound, usually with five leaflets of which the three terminal ones are the largest. The total leaf maybe as long as 14 inches! In the fall these turn a rich, golden hue, and it is then that the hickory tree is most conspicuous. The uniformly pumpkin-colored leaves define the scraggly tall, slim silhouette of the shagbark hickory, which we may have overlooked in the summertime since it usually grows in association with other, more common hardwoods. This is the only species of hickory tree which is native to Maine and even it is not common in our state except in southern counties. But quite a few of them are observable, especially in autumn and winter, as one drives along the Maine turnpike or Route 295 from Brunswick to Kittery. Also, there are some between Wiscasset and Bath along Route 1.

The wood is flexible, close-grained, and very heavy. These characteristics caused the tree to be too heavily harvested. The pioneers used it for boxes, gun ramrods, fence-rails, barrel hoops, door hinges, and furniture. Rocking-chairs of hickory wood with seats and backs of woven hickory splints still grace the wide verandas of old country inns. I remember with nostalgia the hickory wood furniture on our Girl Scout camp porch: rocker, straight chairs, a settee, a table.

But probably more hickory wood was burned than used in any kind of construction. Providing long-lasting coals, a cord of seasoned hickory wood is almost equal to a ton of anthracite, and the green wood is unsurpassed as a source of coals and fumes for the smoking of hams. We hope to have a Pennsylvania hickory-smoked ham this winter.

Despite all these reasons for its destruction, the shagbark hickory survives as a fine nut-bearing tree and as an important member of the central hardwood forest. It's a slow-growing tree which may live for us to 250 years. The largest *carya ovata* in Maine is in Kittery, 80 feet high, 9 ft., 6 in. in circumference. Although it does not mature until almost 80 years of age, it then produces up to two bushels of nuts annually and these are relished by squirrels, wild turkeys, foxes, mice—and humans!

Nov. 29, 1984

HYPERACTIVE WEASEL

"What little animal, squirrel-size, I'd say, but slimmer, can I have seen from my window? It was principally whitish in color, but there were brown areas also. And it moved very rapidly! The inquiry was from East Boothbay's beloved Harold Clifford. The date was close to Feb. 15, 1976. I had often received calls about birds, but seldom about mammals.

John and I had both picked up the telephone and we answered simultaneously. John: "An ermine!" I: "A weasel!" We were both correct. John had used the furrier's term, I, the zoologist's.

The weasels, active in all parts of North America, have, like the snowshoe hare, the characteristic of changing pelage. In winter, the coat is all white except for the tip of the tail, which is black. It is excellent camouflage. And there's even a pelagial adjustment to the zone in which there may or may not be significant snowfall, some individuals changing to white in winter, some remaining brown. This is apparently nature's provision that some weasels will survive, whether it be a white winter or not.

The winter pelt, white with black tail-tip, is the traditional ermine fur of royalty; it is strikingly handsome against a regal, purple robe. Scientists believe that the change in pelage is triggered by lengthening or shortening days, rather than by temperature. This theory would account for

the fact that the weasel observed in East Boothbay was already changing to its summer coat.

In the same family as weasels, *mustelidae*, are the mink, the black-footed ferret, the river and sea otters, the marten, the wolverine, the skunk, the fisher, and the badger. Many of these are right here in the Boothbays and throughout Lincoln County. Although seldom seen, all of these mammals are important to the wildlife community. The fisher, for instance, is considered beneficial to forests because it preys upon porcupines.

The weasel eats animal matter entirely, and prefers its meat at "blood heat" and "quivering". It wants its mouse-steak "rare"! A fierce and persistent hunter, driven, it is thought, by a relentless nervous tension rather than by insatiable hunger, the weasel kills and eats rodents, birds, rabbits, snakes, frogs, even eggs, and insects. Unlike most mammals which are either diurnal or nocturnal, the weasel will hunt by day or night. Lithe, strong, its muscles marvelously coordinated this relatively small mammal possesses a fearless speed and an amazing killing technique (piercing the victim's skull with its canines). Thus equipped, the weasel dares to attack prey much larger than itself—snowshoe hare, for example. Although he, too, will raid a chicken coop, the weasel is an effective enemy of the Norway rat, notorious pest of the poultry farm. Although he has been known to hoard food, "it would have to be a lean winter indeed for the weasel, who loves the taste of fresh, warm blood, to resort to carrion."

And what likes to eat the weasel? Hawks, owls, larger mammals, and large snakes will prey upon the weasel if they can—the white ermine, when there is no snow on the ground, is in danger of attack from these natural enemies. And, men still set traps for weasels.

In late April or early May, the female weasel will give birth to a litter of from four to eight or more tiny infants—pink, wrinkled, nearly naked, blind, each weighing less than an ounce. She had mated last summer, the kits of her last litter barely independent—or perhaps she herself had been only three or four months old. The den in which the babies are born will be in open woodland. Whether the nest is newly made or recycled, it will be softly and warmly lined with fur—not ermine fur, but mouse or rabbit fur. When the kits are two weeks old, the father will bring meat to supplement their milk diet. They'll grow rapidly, be weaned at five weeks of age, and ready to leave the den when seven or eight weeks old. In that short time they'll have frolicked with each other and with their mother, and they'll have learned how to feed and protect themselves. Inexperienced, some of them will meet with disaster, but some will grow up to be indefatigable, alert, active mammals, filling an important niche in our ecology.

November 30, 1995

WINTER

All still and softly through the night
The snow fell hushed and pure and white,
Each branch and twig is laden high,
Outlined against a leaden sky.
Such joy in this white world there lies,
A beauty felt beyond these skies.

—Susan Goldmark

THE OLDSQUAW CHORUS

The flock of oldsquaws on Linekin Bay may be half-way out to Ocean Point but, from our deck which is approximately 400 feet from the shore of the bay, we can hear the chorus. There is something very beautiful about the sound of old-squaws carried across the water. Richard Pough in his *Audubon Water Bird Guide* calls the oldsquaw "a noisy duck at all seasons; the distinctive melodious calls can at times be heard at least a mile." He likens the general effect to "the distant baying of a musical pack of hounds."

Whoever first dubbed these sea-ducks "oldsquaws" had a sense of humor. Any large group of people free to converse—men, women or both—especially if the room is low-ceilinged, can produce a deafening volume of sound. But that cannot approach the clamor of the oldsquaws.

Oldsquaws are sea-ducks. The scientific name of the species is *clangula hyemalis* which is derived from the Latin words *clangor* which means "noise" and *hiems* which means "winter"—so, this is a noisy winter duck, and there's no arguing that point! If you hear the clangor, train your binoculars in that direction and look for the bold dark-and-white pattern so well described in both of the popular bird guides, and also note that some—they are the males—have elongated, needle-like tail-feathers. No other ocean duck has this feature.

This duck is common on Maine's off-shore waters from mid-October through the month of April. A friend reported first seeing one this autumn on Oct. 18, 1984. Many linger here through May. As a general rule the oldsquaws will take off for the far northland just after the loons have left the salt water for Maine's recently thawed inland lakes.

They will fly all the way to the arctic tundra and there, above the treeline, perhaps among sedges near some shallow pond or perhaps near sea water, they will raise their families.

It is reported that oldsquaws like to nest in close association with arctic terns which, in their fierce attacks against the predacious gulls, ravens, and jaegers, offer a protective umbrella to the less aggressive oldsquaws. Even in that open terrain, the nest is exceedingly well concealed. It will be constructed of weed stems, grasses, and bits of leaves. Only dwarf willow and a few shrubs can survive in that environment. Then the mother duck will pluck her breast to provide down and soft feathers to line the nursery. The pale, buffy eggs —probably six but possibly more—are devotedly incubated, almost surely by just the female, who will continue to add down to the floor of the nest during the 24 to 26 days of incubation.

When newly hatched, the baby ducklings will swim, dive, bob, and duck in the shallow nearby water. Lessons from the mother will include how to find their own food and how to escape from predators. While they are small the greatest threat to their lives is from glaucous gulls. In *Wild America* Roger Tory Peterson writes of observing 15 oldsquaw ducklings in the care of one mother. Later, when movies of this large family group were shown to Peter Scott, that ornithologist remarked, "Oh, it's pretty certain, though of course unprovable, that you've got two broods there; it's a very common things among the sea-ducks—the pooling of broods under one joint mother-cum-foster-mother." We notice the same situation among the eiders which, in late May and June, we can watch from our Maine shores. Sometimes there's a cluster of twenty or more ducklings, and several female adults on duty—we call the extra adults "aunts". There's safety in numbers!

Whatever arrangements the oldsquaws make, they do manage to maintain a stable population. Eskimos rob their nests of down for garments and of eggs for food, but this perdition does not seem significant. If not too much is taken and if the timing is right the birds can replace both eggs and down. These ducks are not table favorites since they are considered both tough and "fishy"; therefore they are seldom gunned down by hunters.

The adult oldsquaws can and at times do dive to depths of 200 feet for fish but more commonly they obtain amphipods, shrimps, crabs, and other small shellfish at moderate depths. The young ducks subsist principally on insect larvae found in pools. Since the northland is noted for its throngs of insects, there must be ample food for the ducklings.

The youngsters will be 35 days old before they can fly but after the first flight progress is rapid. In what seems an incredibly short time they are big enough, strong enough, and self-sufficient enough to accompany their parents and other adults of their kind to our Maine coastal waters. Although many other water birds—the osprey and the double-crested cormorant, for examples, find our shores far too rugged for winter living, the active, noisy oldsquaws bob around in the cold sea. They seem to find it quite a suitable environment for the months between late October and late May. Then—off for cooler territory! When we used to take a birding trip to the New Jersey shore in winter, it was considered a real find to spot a small flock of oldsquaws. Sometimes a few even go as far south as the coast of the Carolinas but if you really want to see oldsquaws in winter—come to Maine!

"Oldsquaws are my favorite ducks," writes Carlton Ogburn in "The Adventure of Birds". "Little Eskimos with heads that look furry, like seal's skin, close up, they are the most active of all our anserines. When not diving—and they have been caught in a net at the incredible depth of 200 feet—they are likely to wheel away in a sportive flight, getting off fast and hurtling over the water on limber wings: it is a puzzle that a bird so chunky at rest can be so lithe in the air. It goes with their liveliness to be garrulous, and the nasal tooting of a flock is audible from afar, like the honking of diminutive geese."

Dec. 6, 1984

A CHARMING NEIGHBOR

We were well aware, even before we had moved into our home, that one of our neighbors, sharing with us the beauty, the shade, the fragrance of this pine-and-spruce dominated woodland bordering Linekin Bay, was the red squirrel. He greeted us—so it seemed—with a scolding tirade. Did he fear we would fell one more cone-laden tree so vital to his existence? We had disturbed the character of the site as little as possible, but every new house means less natural woodland. That was in 1973.

Actually, the red squirrel, was probably defending his hard-won feeding territory from the intrusion of another red squirrel. This species of tree squirrel, sometimes called spruce squirrel or pine squirrel, claims up to four acres of forest land for the support of himself and his family. Within this acreage the home territory is approximately two hundred square yards. It accommodates the winter and summer homes as well as the carefully obtained hoards of food.

Our red squirrel soon accepted us—and the sunflower seeds we had intended for the birds! I suppose it's a reasonable bargain—fewer spruce cones, more sunflower seeds—peaceful coexistence is possible! A human neighbor, speaking of the wildlife displaced as homes are erected, remarked "Poor creatures, they were here first!" But basically Tallwood remains wooded, dominated by high white pine trees, under which grow white and red spruces, balsam fir, white birch, and sapling red oaks. The natural forest floor, thick with evergreen needles, supports an abundance and variety of wildflowers, mushrooms, ferns, mosses, and groundpines. The red squirrel, along with many other wild creatures, can live well here.

Tamiascuriurus hudsonicus is this active little animal's impressive, scientific name. The very large *scuiridae* family of rodents, includes all tree and flying squirrels as well as the ground squirrel (the chipmunk), woodchuck, marmot, and prairie dog. Scuirius means shadetail! The gray squirrel and the fox squirrel, also denizens of the eastern forest, do not carry the word "*tamius* in their scientific names. The reason is that those squirrels never tunnel. The burrowing chipmunk is named *tamius* and our red squirrel resorts to tunneling (usually through snow) just enough to be named *tamias-curius*. The *hudsonicus* part of his scientific name denotes his geographical range. He has been called "Hudson's Bay squirrel."

In the autumn season and in the proceeding summer months the red squirrel is a loner—a very busy loner. He's laying up provisions for the cold winter months ahead. Tirelessly, he traverses the horizontal boughs of the pine and spruce trees, especially in the two hours after sunrise and again before sunset. We have watched him make repeated trips over the same route—fast and without treasure in one direction; on the return trip he is more careful and carries a spruce cone in his mouth. On a ledge of rock we have found his workshop. When our daughter, Fran, was a little girl and we'd come upon a mass of acorn shells in the deciduous woodland of Allentown Pennsylvania's South Mountain, she'd call the spot "a squirrel's dining-room." That was probably so, for the gray squirrel stashes his food for tomorrow singly. And they are more gregarious. Perhaps they'd had a party on that rock! But the red squirrel stores his hoards in two or three caches, the seeds and nuts extracted first from the cones and shells. The pile of shucks is the waste heap. Also, he stores fungi, mushrooms, etc. to vary the winter's diet—but such soft items he "cures" first by allowing them to dry in tree crotches. On our property, the hoards seem to be stashed just below the ground level, in rock crevices. Even with the larder well stocked, he'll remain active all winter except during severe storms.

Mating season for red squirrels is late winter and early spring—late February through March. The female prepares the nest—a bulky structure among tree branches near the trunk or perhaps in a tree cavity. After a gestation period of

38 days, the babies, usually four or five but sometimes as many as seven, are born furless, blind, quite helpless. They will soon grow some downy fur but will remain blind for about four weeks and will be nursed for at least five weeks. I was not able to find out whether or not the father brings food to his mate during this long period. But I did find a recorded observation that the parents, once the young are old enough to be active, play with the babies—and with each other. Wouldn't it be fun to witness this family at play?

South of Canada there may be a second litter. The nest would have to be a new one, for squirrel housekeeping is untidy and unsanitary. The summer home is airy, loosely composed of dried leaves. Their population follows the rhythm of the fructification of the spruce trees; when the cone crop is heavy there will be a population explosion of red squirrels. When it is very light, some squirrels will seek new feeding territories, but many will die. Nomadic finches can fly to a new food supply; squirrels can't.

Although natural enemies of our larger mammals have not survived except in deep wilderness areas, there are plenty of natural enemies for the red squirrel to fear. The marten and the fisher are vicious predators and he is often the victim of the barred owl and the goshawk. If he successfully evades these enemies in his youth he may live to the ripe old age of ten years.

True, he relishes a bird egg now and then in the springtime and also, if he cannot find suitable housing in the natural environment he may invade an attic. But he is part of the wildlife community of the coniferous forest. We consider him a charming and amusing neighbor.

Dec. 3. 1981

ACROBATIC LITTLE CHICKADEE

My First Column in the *Boothbay Register*, 1973.

Dec. 16, 1993: The Acrobatic Little Chickadee is the title I used for my very first You Can Find It Wild *article printed for a Maine paper. That was on Oct. 23, 1973—20 years ago. This with some judicial cropping to conserve space is that article.*

The acrobatic little chickadee is probably the most universally popular of all bird-feeder visitors. They swing, they sway, upside-down or rightside-up. They cheerfully and energetically "chick-dee-dee-dee" all day long. They are the first to investigate in a new feeder; they come to meet us impatiently when we approach to restock it with seeds. Even without invitation they will perch on our shoulders, and with a little encouragement they will eat from our hands and even our lips. Perhaps we respond to the chickadee with affection because he likes us. He seems to understand, to know, that we are friendly, generous, helpful. Who doesn't like to be appreciated?

Most of us know the chickadee as a winter resident. But, actually, they are non-migratory birds. They flock, of course, in winter, moving from one food source to another. If there is not an adequate supply near the summer breeding territory, they will search as far as necessary to find one. Cold weather does not compel them to move, except indirectly. The colder the weather, the more they must eat to fuel their high-powered metabolism. Even when the bird is asleep, the tiny chickadee heart beats 500 times in one minute—more than six times as often as our own. When he's active the rate is about doubled! The little bird, well armed from within, is well insulated from without by several layers of loose, fluffy feathers. So—provided with enough food, he's well set for a rugged winter.

The black-capped chickadee is "our" chickadee. It is the state bird of both Maine and Massachusetts and its range includes the whole northern part of our country. "Our" chickadee has a southern cousin, the Carolina chickadee, and a northern cousin, the boreal chickadee. The southern species is seldom seen north of Pennsylvania. But the northern chickadee is a year-round resident of Maine, although it is uncommon in this Lincoln County area. However, especially if we should have a very severe winter, "it may be seen in small numbers in central and coastal Maine" (*A Birder's Guide to the Coast of Maine*, by Elizabeth and Jan Pierson). Old-time birders called this the brown-capped chickadee. Check your field guide.

With no help at all from us, the black-capped chickadees find an amazingly wide variety of food. In the winter the diet will consist of approximately 50 percent animal food, 50 percent plant food. The animal material will include larvae and eggs of ants, beetles, moths, spiders, wasps, and flies. They eat masses of eggs from which the destructive tent caterpillars would emerge. They like the eggs of the dreaded sawfly, and even the tiny eggs of plant-lice do not escape their careful perusal. In plant food the seeds of hemp, sunflower, pine, pumpkin, and squash are favorites, but those of blueberry, birch, fir, hemlock, oak, serviceberry, spruce, elm, staghorn sumac, Virginia creeper, and poison ivy are also consumed.

Probably the chickadee's only disservice to humans is the spreading of poison ivy seeds whose berries he eats and later eliminates with the seeds not only intact but coated with fertilizer! In addition to the foods they can forage from the wild, they delight in sunflower seeds, bread, peanuts, suet, and mixed small seeds.

From our living room we can watch them at a cage-type hanging feeder (with a block of suet in it) and also on a raised platform feeder. They do not seem to be comfortable feeding from the ground or the deck floor. But the feeders are really for our own enjoyment. Clearly they'd fare very well without our offerings.

Before we know it, we'll be hearing their clear, two- or three-noted whistle, sometimes referred to as their "phoebe" call. Behavior patterns will change as pairing and nesting needs become paramount. Some chickadees accept bird houses but most prefer to retire to a secluded site for the important process of raising a family. Those of us who have clusters of evergreen trees have a good chance of having nesting chickadees near our homes.

Welcome, chickadees, to our feeders!

Dec. 16, 1993

CHRISTMAS BOUQUET

Today I bring you a Christmas bouquet. In it are twigs of bayberry, a sprig or two of holly, and fronds of Christmas fern. Strands of ground-pine bind it together, and a few sprays of balsam fir frame it and provide that wonderful Christmas perfume.

To prepare this bouquet I've extracted Christmas fact and fancy from earlier articles. The bouquet is pretty, fragrant, and it should hold, fresh and green, through the holidays.

The Bayberry: *"A bayberry candle burned to the socket*
Brings luck to the house and gold to the pocket."
The couplet is an old folk-verse. The most important contribution of the bayberry shrub to American life has been as a source of candle wax. The bayberry candle, whether molded or dipped, had superior qualities. It burned slowly and with delightful incense which was accentuated when the candle was snuffed. Furthermore, it did not droop in a hot room as did the candles made from animal tallow. Bayberries were so highly valued in colonial days that a 15-shilling fine was imposed on those who gathered the berries before autumn. As very special Christmas souvenirs from America, twigs of the berries were often sent to England where the bayberry became known as the "tallow shrub" of the New World. And in this New World, the bayberry candle became the symbol of Christmas. In England they burned the Yule-log; in America we burned the bayberry candle.

The Holly: To "deck the halls with boughs of holly" is a custom which reaches far back into pagan times. Respected, available, at its height of beauty in December, the prickly-leaved, red-berried evergreen tree was associated with Yule festivals long before the birth of Christ. Druids, those early

Gallic and British priests, believed that the sun itself was within the glossy leaves and bright berries; they used the plant to ward off evil spirits. Country folk, too, accorded it magical properties. They regarded its shiny foliage as protection against witches. The seven-day Roman Saturnalia celebration occurred at the time of the winter solstice and observed the triumph of light over darkness. Later, Christian leaders, recognizing a compatibility of that theme and Christ's message, placed Christmas at the time of year when the days were beginning to lengthen. For awhile the pagan practice of decorating temples and houses with holly and other evergreens was forbidden to Christians. Eventually this pleasant custom was embraced even to the point that church doors were garlanded with boughs of the spiny leaves and red berries, indicating sanctuary. Monks called the plant "holy tree" and it was considered symbolic of Christ's life—the white flowers signified purity, the red berries His blood; the prickly leaves were the crown of thorns. "Of all the trees that are in the wood, the holly bears the crown."

Christmas Fern: Of the several evergreen ferns native to our New England woodlands none is more handsome than the Christmas fern. The tips of its fronds, which may be up to twenty inches long, protrude through the snow. They are leathery in texture and a shiny, dark green, and of the same structure as the well known Boston house-fern. The Christmas fern is so named because it has been used in large quantities for Christmas wreaths and decorations. On a small scale, and with the fronds carefully cut, not pulled, there's probably no harm in this. Sterile fronds, all year round, enhance any bouquet. The fern's much taller western relative, the sword fern, which grows abundantly in the state of Washington, is the fern which is now sold commercially throughout the country. Only the top two feet of the fronds are harvested with special knives and they continue to grow luxuriantly.

Ground-pine: Great masses of one or another of the club-mosses still flourish in some forested areas of coastal Maine. Although they are popularly used for Christmas wreaths and garlands and for decking the halls with "pine rope" this is a mistake because the *lycopodiums* are becoming rare. These plants propagate themselves by means of creeping or running, establishing new roots as they move along. If left alone in a suitable environment a plant will spread, its own growth dying at a slower rate than that at which the new advances. But the roots are shallow and easily pulled up. Yank at one piece of running pine and you can pull long "ropes" of it—all the way back to where there is no life in the long root-stock. A few more tugs and your arms may be full of ground pine—but the ground at your feet is bare of it. This is not a flowering plant; it bears no seeds. Instead, as with ferns, there are enormous quantities of minute spores. The life cycle of the *lycopodiums* is complex and requires nearly twenty years from spore to mature plant. Let's leave it where we find it beautifying the woodland trailsides.

Balsam: On Christmas Eve the balsam fir is the finest tree of all. Its structure is perfect for use as a Christmas tree. Its trunk is slender and topped by a spire; it is the most symmetrical of all New England evergreens, and its lustrous, dark-green foliage is dense—and very fragrant. The balsam's needles are blunt, comfortable to our touch, and they remain on the twig for weeks after the tree has been brought into the house. We seldom see cones of the balsam fir. Held erect on high branches of mature trees, they disintegrate before they fall. The scales contain the seeds, some of which are eaten by grouse and other woodland creatures. But most of them are blown to hospitable areas where they germinate and start saplings for future Christmas trees. It is wonderful that this fragrant, lovely tree happens to be the most abundant tree in our Maine woods.

MERRY CHRISTMAS!

Dec. 21, 1989

THE PROMISE OF SPRING

A deciduous tree in wintertime, "its branches black and bare", has much to teach us and to give us. Each twig on every tree, each bud on every twig, holds the promise of spring, of the new cycle already underway. What discussion could be more appropriate for New Year's Day?

Each tree species has its own characteristic silhouette, more apparent in wintertime. It's fun to play a game with one's self or to compete with one's companions at recognizing trees from increasing distances. That tree in the open field—is it white birch? A red oak? An aspen? With practice it is possible to identify many trees by their silhouettes, and as we become adept at it there's a pleasant feeling of real acquaintance. Ah, I know you, red oak tree. Without seeing your pointed-lobed leaves, without checking the color of your twigs, without any close observation at all, I know you.

When we begin to play this game we must, it's true, go up close to the tree in order to prove ourselves right or wrong. Now, without a leaf on a twig, and with the ground beneath it snow-covered so that we can't search for fallen leaves or fruits, there are many clues as to the tree's identity.

With some, the bark is so distinctive that we know immediately what it is—a white birch, a beech, a red-osier dogwood. Each tree species has its typical twigs with recognizable characteristics such as thickness, degree of smoothness, color, odor, taste, leaf scars, arrangement of buds.

The buds are the best clue of all, and the most inspiring. For, here within a small, compact, well protected bundle is next summer's leaf or flower. And although not any two individual buds are identical, each tree can be recognized by its buds. The gleaming, brown-gold buds of the beech tree, for instance, are long and slender, the buds of the American hornbeam tree are tiny, about 1/8th inch long, and covered with brown, white-edged scales. Some buds, poplar for one, have gummy coats.

When this column had just begun, an Allentown (Pa.) reader wrote, "It was only last winter that I really looked and took time to observe buds on trees, and so I've come to know and love especially the beautiful, golden-flecked buds on the butternut hickory and the unusual, angled bud of the black oak." With very little practice you can tell the difference between flower buds and leaf buds. To start with flowering shrubs is a good way. Any of us who has a rhododendron shrub can count, now, how many clusters of blossoms there will be on that shrub next spring (or summer, if it's rhododendron maximum). A phrase I like to quote is Bill Reimert's, "A dogwood tree never keeps its secrets very well."

With a great diversity in shapes, sizes, and types of coverings, all buds have devices for retaining moisture which should stay in, and for repelling the snow and ice and wind. Later, when spring comes and the leaves push their protections aside, it is revealed that there is also a great variety of methods for the enfolding of that leaf or flower within its case and also for the unfolding from it. With some, as the outermost sheath is thrust back by the life force within it, we see that as one neatly folded leaf is released another or even several more were held within that bud.

Tree buds are often favorite winter foods for wild creatures. Grouse and ptarmigan feed on alder buds. Birch buds are relished by many wildfowl. In *Homeland*, Hal Borland reports that partridges eat apple buds—but not until late February, when "the whole urgency of the apple tree begins to assert itself —and the partridges know it, even though I don't until the partridges tell me." He suggests that perhaps the birds need a vitamin which the apple bud develops at that time. At any rate, it holds true for him that if he cuts apple twigs to force before the partridges come to eat the buds, no blossoms develop. Twigs cut for forcing after those birds have helped themselves to some of them, do produce blossoms!

To consider the intricacies of winter twigs and buds can not only teach us some lessons in natural science, but also

sharpen our reverence for the marvel and mystery of life.
I wish every reader a Very Happy New Year!

Dec. 30, 1993

CROW CAPERS

The common crow, *corvus brachyrhnchos*, is admired for his cleverness and his vocal versatility; he is maligned as a corn-thief, deplored as a nest-robber, and respected for his adaptability.

Enough crows stay in Maine all winter for this species to be listed as 'common' throughout the year. However the great majority of the crows we have in spring and summer and fall do fly to warmer places in wintertime. In these warmer overwintering locations (areas of Chesapeake Bay, for instance, they congregate in enormous flocks—up to hundreds of thousands). In such situations they are considered obnoxious and may even actually be a menace to the resident humans and wildlife. But here we welcome the bold black bird and feel a respect for his decision to stick it out in his home territory.

Those that remain in our area during the cold months of the year can't have an easy time of it. Described as omniverous, there is just about no food they won't eat or can't adjust to—insects, reptiles, rodents, seeds (notably corn), fruits, birds' eggs and nestlings, fish and carrion. A rabbit or squirrel killed on the highway is likely to be cleaned up by crows. But virtually no insects, reptiles, rodents are available, dead or alive these days. Certainly there are no bird eggs or nestlings. Wild seeds are probably consumed, and some people report crows at their feeders. One problem for them at feeders, even if welcome, is that seeds for the small birds should be dry. The crow likes, or needs, to have his seeds moist. That's why he relishes corn after it's been planted!

I remember that on a January day in a colder winter than this one, I was barred from the Linekin beach near our home by a veritable glacier. But, as I looked down upon the array of ice-platters scattered about the sand, one large bird animated the cold picture. He flew low over the water toward shore, then lifted and perched on a dock-post. He had chosen a spot in the sun which made his black plumage gleam and which must have warmed his body, as it did my face.

The bird was the common crow and I suppose that in wintertime a crow can find the best livelihood right along the water. Dead sea creatures are washed ashore and among the seaweeds and tidepools at low tide there is much life which the crow can obtain. He may even resort to catching his own fish. His cousin, the fish crow, (not this far north) is adept at this skill. But it's not an easy life!

Come spring it's another story. When the gang returns from the southern resorts, there'll be a period of flocking here, the migrators mingling raucously with the rugged individuals who stayed at home. Then gradually there'll be a pairing and a fanning out into family territories. Crows, although they may feed gregariously, are not colonial nesters. At this point the crows are quiet and reclusive.

The nest will be placed high in an evergreen tree and, although from below it will appear slipshod and awkward, its construction is sound. It will serve the family well for this season, and next year will be strong enough to provide the foundation for an owl or hawk nest.

On the nest's soft grass lining, the female will deposit several, probably five, well camouflaged eggs, greenish and probably splotched with gray or brown. After a period of from 15 to 18 days, the incubation chore shared by both parents, the nestlings will be reared on a diet composed entirely of animal matter, principally insects. It has been determined that one family of crows devours about 40,000 insects in one season. After all, it's a fairly large brood, the crow is a large bird and so is its appetite. The youngsters are in the nest for a long period—between four and five weeks. In 35 days five growing crows demand a lot of food and the parents want them to have the best protein diet—that means insects!

During this period the parents are ready, willing and able to steal, for their own consumption, the eggs and nestlings of other birds—small songbirds, field birds like pheasants, and water birds. In his beautiful book, *Birds of North America, a Personal Selection*, Elliot Porter tells of personally observing a crow with an eider's egg, which is large and strong-shelled!

What are the crow's enemies? The hawks and the owls will rob crow's nests when they can. So would a snake—which may be why the crow's nest is high. But crows are credited with exceptional ability to cope with their problems. It is well recognized, for instance, that crows have an alarm call. It has been verified that neighboring crows will respond to it and, with mob action, drive off an owl, even kill it.

Members of the crow family (*corvidae*) of which the ravens are the largest and the jays most brightly colored, are considered to be the most intelligent of all birds. Their brains are proportionately larger than the brains of any other bird group. Crows adjust quickly to changing conditions. They can distinguish between a man and a stick and a man with a gun. Captive crows have proven that they can count (up to three or four) and that they can solve puzzles. They can associate sounds and symbols with food and they actually seem to have a language all their own. They can also mimic other birds and even human voice. They have learned to drop a clam from a height onto rock so that the shell breaks. Gulls do that also but often drop the treasure onto sand. Crows have a much higher rate of success with that trick which approaches the use of a tool.

So the crow is a bird to admire. Enjoy the crows this winter! John Madson expresses his feeling for overwintering crows this way; "When bluebirds and swallows return, I will always welcome them with relief and affection—but never with the respect that I hold for the crows that never went."

Feb. 10, 1983

DEN TREES

Den trees: that's the term foresters use for the large dead trees obviously occupied by various forms of wildlife. They and naturalists recognize that den trees offer valuable service to wildlife and thus to the environment. The birds which nest in dead trees are the very ones whose feeding habits are the greatest help to living trees. Up and down the trunks they go—the nuthatches, the woodpeckers—all four seasons of the year, scouring the bark for adult insects and for their larvae and eggs. The mammals, too, have their own important niches. The fisher keeps the porcupine in control; the fox consumes large quantities of rodents, and so it goes—all of them necessary for a balanced, natural ecology.

One simple 5-word sentence will answer all of the following questions. What is it that the bluebird, the honeybee, the flying squirrel, some of the bats, and the goldeneye duck do which the robin, the woodchuck, and the loon do not? How is a chickadee like a raccoon? What trait do the following creatures have in common: the tiny red-breasted nuthatch, the kestrel, the tree swallow, the screech owl, and the porcupine? In what way are carpenter ants like the wood duck?

The answer to all of those riddles is—They all like to nest in tree cavities. Starlings, the barred and saw whet owls, both of the nuthatches, the Carolina and winter wrens, the tufted titmouse also nest in cavities and so does the popular little bufflehead duck.

We don't have to own a large tract of land to be able to contribute to suitable living conditions for wild creatures. Many of us own a couple of acres which we have allowed to develop naturally. If those acres include some mature live trees and also at least one dead one, the wild population will be quite diverse. Under the big trees there are saplings and also under-story trees (such as hawthorn and dogwood) and there are shrubs (perhaps barberry, witchhazel, and winter-berry). There are herbaceous plants like the wood asters and ferns and ground-cover plants like wintergreen, wild lily-of-the-valley, bunchberry, and partridgeberry. Throughout such a tract there will be nesting sites, food and shelter for all forms of animal life. Maine alone has 29 species of birds and 19 mammals known to utilize den trees—some during the nesting season, some during the winter. And those species like to find food nearby!

Near our home there's a large, old decaying yellow birch tree. The series of holes in its trunk indicates that in the decade or so since the tree last bore leaves it has been home to several species of birds. My guess would be that black-capped chickadees, downy and hairy woodpeckers have occupied those cavities. Surely the tree has been host to a colony of carpenter ants. Perhaps flying squirrels have been tenants in a hole first carved out by flickers. It could be that the honeybees which pollinate the flowers in the nearby gar-den have their hive in that tree.

Not far away is a tall, slender, dead pine tree which has a tiny round hole near its gaunt, weather-silvered top. A few years ago I watched a red-breasted nuthatch ferry food into that hole. I shuddered to think of the first hazardous venture the fledglings would make from that high cavity with noth-ing between them and the earth, some 60 feet below. Downy woodpeckers might take over that hole, enlarge it, and cus-tomize it for their own use. If the tree were a very large one, perhaps the victim of lightening, still larger birds might use it in successive years. We once saw a tree skeleton in which the largest of many cavities was occupied by a pileated woodpecker family.

Tom Fegely, writing in his wildlife column in Pennsylva-nia, hopes that "an awareness of the importance of den trees...will help assure that the demand for firewood in coming years won't cause a housing shortage in the wildlife world."

Dec. 11, 1997

DESIGNED FOR WINTER

During this winter's record-setting cold temperatures, combined with deeper-than-usual snow accumulation, we've been asked how the birds and wild mammals manage to cope with this kind of weather. "Where do they sleep?" "How do they keep warm enough?", "Won't they freeze?"

For today we'll limit the discussion to the problems which severe weather presents to birds.

Where do birds sleep in wintertime? Many of them sleep in cavities. We have a chickadee which, when it comes to the feeder in the early morning, has a crooked tail. It must have spent the night cramped into a small hole, perhaps a wrenhouse or maybe a know-hole. Brush piles, especially if insulated by snow, and the densely needled boughs of young evergreens offer snug roosts to sparrows and finches. The woodpeckers and nuthatches retreat to the cavities in which they or others nested. The little brown creeper, whose nest was hidden beneath a strip of loose bark, finds some such cover, protected from wind, in which to sleep.

If there is snow the ruffed grouse is all set. It plunges, headfirst, into a soft snowbank, shapes a recess not much larger than itself, and sleeps, warmly blanketed. There, under perhaps two feet of snow, the bird's own body heat raises the temperature of the shelter by as much as 60° F. Several of these birds may occupy the same bank, but each will have its own hole—no communal bedding, although they may form an outward-facing circle. In the morning each grouse will walk to the top of the bank, beat its wings against the snow for takeoff, and fly to the nearest food supply. If the partridgeberries, wild cranberries, wintergreen, and other food on the ground is locked away from them, the grouse will find nourishment in tree buds. In this area a favorite tree is the yellow birch whose buds have the same refreshing, wintergreen flavor as do the forest-floor plants of the same name.

In *The Birds of Winter,* Kit and George Harrison call their first chapter "Designed for Winter". They tell us of various devices that have evolved and strategies that are practiced which aid birds in coping with severe winter weather. Have you noticed that birds seem to be larger on cold days? A bird's skin has tiny muscles which can raise the feathers, thus trapping air which, as a down puff does for us, serves as an insulating layer of body-warmed air. Furthermore, the plumage of many birds actually does have up to 30 percent more feathers in winter than in summertime. And there's a "counter-current heat exchange system" which keeps the legs and feet of many birds reasonably freeze-resistant.

Still another adaptation to frigid weather occurs during the long winter nights. Some birds, perhaps most of those that survive the coldest nights, become torpid, with lowered body temperature and reduced heartbeats. Hypothermia, for them, is actually a conservation of energy. Although humans, to survive, must maintain a body temperature of within a very few degrees, birds tolerate a much wider range. And, there is entirely reliable evidence that some birds snuggle together in a cavity, sharing body warmth.

No, it is not the cold which is the determining factor as to whether a bird will spend the winter here and whether it will survive if it does. The availability of suitable food is what is critical. Almost all songbirds raise their young on a diet of insects. Exceptions are goldfinch which feed their babies a sort of pablum—regurgitated, semi-digested seeds. Those species which cannot adapt to a winter diet of seeds, dried fruits or dormant insects must fly to where they can find food similar to their summer fare. Owls, hawks, and shrikes (predatory birds) require meat the year around, but they are equipped to secure mice and other flesh usually available throughout the winter. The water birds that require a year-round diet of fish, must move southward to where freshwater is open—or move to the ocean.

In her very fine and beautiful article, *Thus They Shall Survive*, Louise de Kiriline Lawrence tells us in the Jan. 1972 issue of *Audubon* magazine that "...for all of the birds it held true that the cooler the night, the later they left their roosts, and the shorter was their day because they went to roost earlier. The extension of the long night and fast seemed an anomaly." Yet, she noted that the only birds to succumb were the weaklings and then not directly to cold but to predators. A few of those individuals became life-saving food for a barred owl which moved in closer to the feeder. The small rodents it would have liked to catch and eat were safe in their underground tunnels. Two martens and a red fox competed with the owl for the few snowshoe hares that were about that winter. And the bluejays gave the owl a hard time in the feeding-station area!

Jan. 27, 1994

FOR THE BIRDS...SUET

Creating your own suet cakes is easy and inexpensive. You'll need: Beef suet (bought at the store, or trimmings, saved over time in the freezer); plastic tubs or small cans (such as margarine, tuna); and a combination of cornmeal and peanut butter, bird seed (millet, hulled sunflowers, cracked corn); raisins and nuts.

Cut beef suet in small pieces. Slowly and carefully melt, removing any remaining chunks. Pour into bowl. Add one part peanut butter, seeds, nuts, etc. and one part cornmeal. Stir until well blended, and pour into tubs or cans. Freeze excess for later use.

THE WILEY RED FOX

Outside our back window is a line of animal footprints. These are fox tracks, almost surely those of the red fox. Although the snow is more than two feet deep a crust supported the animal and the topmost, new fallen inch of snow reveals a recognizable trail. A fox print, like a dog's, shows four toe-prints which are staggered. The fox's prints follow in a straight course (except where he has deviated, perhaps to investigate a new scent). Also, they are narrower than a dog's in proportion to the length which, depending upon whether the print is left in snow or mud or sand, varies from one and three-quarter inch to two and one-half inches. As a fox walks it sweeps its tail with every step. If these whisk marks are evident, it's certain proof that the trail is not a dog's.

Early February is courtship and mating time for the fox. Their sharp, staccato barks may rouse us in the middle of the night and this is the time of year, too, when we are most likely to see the animal during the day. We've heard the barking and what fun it would be to watch the mate circle around his chosen vixen, his way of wooing her!

The vixen prepares the den. Perhaps she digs it herself or perhaps she adapts an old woodchuck hole to her needs. It will have several exists—four, five or even more. We once knew of an entrance, really quite conspicuous under a rock, but never did we discover one of the exits. Although the average adult red fox is about sixteen inches tall, the height of the entrance will be about eight inches. The fox has to squeeze in, in order to enter the tunnel which inside may be quite wide and deep.

The mated foxes den up together and after a fifty-one day gestation period the pups, four to nine of them, will be born. They'll be blind and each will be about the size of a mole. They'll be dark brown (or perhaps gray) and, even at birth, each tail will be white-tipped, a feature common to all of this species, regardless of other color variations (cross, silver, etc.).

The male fox is faithful throughout the period, bringing food to the youngsters and in training them to be self-sufficient. For instance, the pup's first killing experience will probably be with a mouse or small rabbit which a parent has caught but only disabled. After about one month in the den the young foxes small world is gradually enlarged. They play and feed at the den entrance; they take short, escorted trips. They may even be moved to a new den for safety's sake.

Often, as insurance against danger, several spare dens are claimed. These would be within the home range which may cover an area of up to ten square miles.

By autumn the pups will be approximately six months old and they will leave their parents. Some may wander far away from the den of their birth (as much as one hundred miles and even more); others will remain nearby. But each, until next winter will lead an independent, solitary life. They eat omnivorously of wild grapes, berries and other fruits, beetles, grasshoppers, birds, and most of all, rodents, ranging in size from mouse to woodchuck. The greatest threat to birds and their eggs is probably in the spring. Even then the nocturnal habits of the fox dictate that they cannot serve as a major item. An adult fox consumes about one pound of food per day and by far the greatest proportion is of rodents. In this way the foxes, both red and gray, are beneficial species from a humans point of view.

When winter comes they do not hibernate, even when the bitterest winter days are here. Instead, they lead very active lives from dusk until dawn. They do not use a den for sleeping but, instead, the animal curls into a ball, feet and nose protected by the ample, bushy, white-tipped tail. When the weather is good they enjoy sleeping in the winter sunshine!

The months of rugged, active life result in the foxes being in prime physical condition by late winter. Since maximum quality in the offspring is assured by the parents being at their healthiest at the time of conception, the new fox year, starting in early February, is off to a auspicious beginning.

In Sally Carrighar's fascinating book, *Wild Heritage*, she comments on the fact that for most mammals early spring is the ideal time to be born. Our family's doctor made the same observation for human babies. For our species, it means that the most vulnerable months of infancy are past by the time harsh winter weather sets in. Wild mammals must be independent of their parents by autumn even though in some instances, the offspring remain with their mother throughout the first year. Almost all of those mammals which have only one litter per year (therefore excepting many of the rodents) give birth in the springtime—April and May in our area, earlier in the south.

Feb. 19, 1987

NATURAL THERMOMETERS

Those of us fortunate enough to look out from our windows upon rhododendron's have, for the winter months, natural thermometers. On the coldest days the deep-green leaves are tightly curled inward, dangling like pencils from the stout twigs. They are as cold as they appear to be and are employing nature's method of protection. The microscopic holes in the underside of each leaf, called *stomata*, through which the leaf breathes, are thus sheltered from the fiercest, most direct cold.

As the weather becomes warmer, the dark, leathery, glossy leaves lift and unroll, ready to perform their natural functions and, incidentally, letting us know that the temperature is more comfortable. My mother was no naturalist, but she was observant and appreciative. I remember her saying as we prepared to leave for school, "Better bundle up well today; those rhododendron leaves are as tight as nails."

Most of the rhododendron planted as shrubbery is hybrid, probably of Asiatic or European origin. It will bloom earlier but be no more beautiful than the rhododendron maximum, our native shrub. At its most splendid in the southern highlands, where it actually attains tree size and form, it nevertheless is hardy in the north, even in Vermont and Maine.

Maine's Josselyn Botanical Society, named for the early English botanist, records in its 1966 checklist four species of rhododendron and three species of laurel native to our state. Great rhododendron, *r. maximum*, is found wild in four counties: Somerset, Franklin, Cumberland, and York. There are six additional counties where it has been reported but cannot be considered established. Lincoln County is not one of these; but since the hybrid rhododendron is frequently planted here (some thrive at the front of the *Boothbay Register*) and since its cousin, *kalmia latifolia*, mountain laurel, is found here (on Ocean Point Road in East Boothbay and on Elm Street in Damariscota, for instance), we, Heyls, felt reasonably confident that the wild great rhododendron would succeed on our own home property. We planted some which we brought with us from Pennsylvania in 1973. We placed it in well-drained but moist open pine woods in rich, acid-black soil where it receives a heavy natural mulch of pine needles each fall. We've never given it any extra cover and it has, indeed, thrived. Right now it holds seven buds for next summer's flower clusters.

The same mountain streams that the hemlock tree loves, rhododendron favors. Dense thickets of it grow on banks of undisturbed mountain lakes; to walk "through the rhododendron's" on a trail which was probably first opened by deer, and to breathe the clean fragrance always present in that shade, is a lovely and refreshing experience. The peak of the blossoming period is in July, the date depending upon the latitude and the altitude. It will bloom after its hybrid cousins and the lesser rhododendron's and also after the closely related laurels and azaleas have faded. The extraordinarily beautiful flowers are borne in clusters of up to a dozen white through rosy-pink to red blossoms. (Catawba rhododendron and most the hybrid's are purplish.) Botanically perfect, each individual flower bears both pistil and stamens. Nevertheless, it is cross-fertilized by bees, clear-winged moths, and other insects.

Like most members of this family, the nectar of the flowers is poisonous. Bee-masters carefully avoid the honey manufactured during the weeks that the rhododendron is in bloom. But the bees themselves are immune! The leaves of the shrub also are poisonous and generally are avoided by deer. But where they grow in great tangles they offer shelter and protection from predators, including men, to deer and other mammals.

Not all members of the rhododendron family have evergreen leaves. Rhodora and swamp azalea, for instance, do not. But the great rhododendron and the hybrid's do; so do the three laurels native to Maine: mountain, sheep, and pale. Like the holly these are classed as brown-leaved evergreens and the leaves of all of them are responsive to temperature changes.

Now in the depth of winter, close examination of the rhododendron shrub reveals the promise of spring and summer of 1981. Every twig has its leaf buds and some of the terminal buds—bigger, stickier and with more scales—are the flower buds which in springtime will swell until in July the immense buds will burst open with their radiant contribution to our beautiful eastern woodlands. As I mentioned earlier, there are seven of these big flower buds on our own shrub.

In Springvale, Maine, is this state's largest natural stand of great rhododendron. Known now as the Harvey Butler Rhododendron stand, it has been designated as a critical area and is under the protection of the New England Wild Flower Society. The stand is composed of about five acres which includes one very dense impenetrable thicket of 3.3 acres. The NEWFS usually sponsors a trip to this sanctuary in mid-July. We are told that the trail has a few up-and-down hills, with about three-quarters of a mile walk into the rhododendron stand. I'm going to try to go there on next summer's trip.

Jan. 1, 1981

COURTS FIRST, EATS LATER

Recently we discussed how Maine's wild mammals meet the challenges of winter. I pointed out that Maine has few true hibernators—and that the woodchuck *marmota monax,* also known as the groundhog, is our largest and most often seen hibernator.

At this time of year Maine's woodchucks are definitely in hibernation, each adult in his or her own burrow. A young male, born probably last May, weighing only one ounce, blind and naked, will probably weigh seven pounds, and will be well-furred. At about the time of first real frost, having fattened himself on grasses, grains, garden produce, and orchard or wild fruits, the groundhog, a butterball of a rodent by that time, crawls into the burrow (which he may have dug himself). He determines what will be his sleeping room, plugs it tight against intruders and curls up and sleeps "for the duration". Respiration and pulse becomes slow and his body temperature drops to something near 58° F.

Earlier accounts of this rodent suggest that during hibernation he uses up the stored fat and that when he emerges from his den in spring the chuck is very thin and ravenously hungry. It is now believed that the heavy layer of fat was principally for insulation during the long sleep. It will be used to sustain the animal during the time when very little vegetation is available to him and when his greatest urgency is to find a female. To satisfy this need he may wander far. He may fight another male woodchuck, he may face danger from dogs, fishers, owls, and hawks—and he may mate with several females. Often he must dig his way through hard-packed snow to reach her in her den.

Digging is no real problem for a woodchuck. The powerful forelegs, heavy claws, and the large teeth equip this mammal for digging. To watch him you might think he digs for the fun of digging—but there's a purpose to all that activity. Every hole is a part of the burrow-system which will have a front entrance marked by a mound of earth, all of which has been carried out by mouth. The tunnel may be as much as 45 feet long but the earth is all deposited at this front entrance. The mound becomes the woodchuck's observation platform. There are also back and/or side doors, perhaps as many as five. These are unmarked and would be indiscernible to you and me but anyone who has ever watched a spaniel attempt to rout a groundhog knows they exist! There are "rooms" inside the burrow —a nestroom (in a female's burrow), a sleeping room, and a toilet room. And these are well kept. They are occasionally cleaned out and when it becomes damp the bedding of grasses and leaves is changed.

"Courting First, Eating Later" is the caption of one headline in the very good book, *Backyard Wildlife* by Kit and George Harrison. "In a methodical, direct route, he goes from one burrow to another, sniffs at the entrance, and...when he finds a burrow that his nose tells him houses an available female...with tail wagging like an eager puppy, he cautiously enters the burrow. He moves in with her for the duration of their February, March or April courtship. This is the only time of the year when two adult chucks inhabit the same burrow."

Before the young chucks are born, the female ejects him from the burrow and then she does a "spring cleaning job", adapting the winter sleeping room into a nursery. The tiny babies are less than four inches long when they are born, but, nourished by their mother's rich milk, they grow rapidly.

"The woodchuck mothers we've been able to observe", writes Kit Harrison, "seemed to enjoy and be affectionate with their offspring. A woodchuck mother must also be a good tutor, making certain that her family learns well the lessons of survival." By midsummer the mother's burrow is too small for the growing youngsters. They move into nearby burrows, perhaps abandoned by others, perhaps newly excavated by the mother. She keeps a watchful eye out for her youngsters until they and she become independent.

Woodchucks are benign creatures. They prey upon no

member of the animal kingdom—not bird, not insect, not mammal. They are completely herbivorous in their eating— and that's where they conflict with our lives. They like to eat the same vegetable food we like to eat—and they are hungriest during our harvest time.

Jan. 30, 1997

THE ROGUE BLUE JAY

As I've gathered material on the bluejay I've felt as if I were a judge, or at least a juror, charged with the responsibility of weighing a great amount of reliable and convincing evidence for and against the handsome, raucous bird.

Everybody knows the bluejay by sight. Crested, larger than a robin, with striking plumage of bright blue-black-white and gray, dominant and prominent except in the nesting season, he is readily recognized and variously acclaimed. Corn thief! Nest robber! You gorgeous fellow! Brave one! Smaller birds might cry, 'You stole my eggs!' or 'You saved my life!' Farmers may complain: 'You steal my corn!'. Foresters approve, 'You eat the wood-boring beetles and you plant oak trees.'

Let's consider some of the testimony.

John James Audubon, artist-ornithologist of more than one hundred years ago, admitted that the bluejay is a beauty and a cheerful fellow as well, but he berated the bird as selfish, mischievous, and malicious. He described him as a thief, a rogue, a knave. These are words of emotion and ones applied usually only to humans. I do not find recorded observations to substantiate these strong criticisms, but Audubon would have had ample opportunity to 'catch him in the act' when a bluejay raided a smaller bird's nest for egg or baby.

A present day artist, photographer, ornithologist, Eliot Porter, does testify with incriminating evidence of the predations of the bluejay. He has personally observed a bluejay with a still-wriggling red-eyed vireo-nestling dangling from its beak while the distressed parents cried pitifully. He also reports the raiding of a very well hidden brown creeper's nest and of a tree swallow's nest for which he blames the bluejay.

We, Heyls, in our observations of cardinal nests, have never caught him in the act, yet we blame the bluejay for the raiding of more than one such nest. The bluejay seems always to be stealthily lurking in the trees near the place where the cardinals are constructing or tending their first nest of the season and the cardinals do not keep their secret well, always chirping when approaching the nest.

So we'll have to accept as fact the testimony that the bluejays do rob nests of smaller birds. But what about the evidence in their favor?

The jay is highly intelligent as are all members of the crow family which includes magpies and ravens as well as crows and jays. Roger Tory Peterson writes in *How to Know the Birds* that it has been "predicted that when man, through his ingenuity, has finally destroyed all his neighbors and himself too, there will still be crows." For a demonstration of his intelligence just note how quickly he solves the problems of how to get the food you thought you were keeping from him! And, speaking of feeders, although he is clever, gluttonous, one of his champions, Dr. William J. Long, claims that he is much less scrappy and rude than the junco!

Stomach analysis has found that 76 percent of the jays' food is vegetable material (acorns, beechnuts, corn, and other seeds and fruits). He stashes most of the acorns, many of them beneath leaves on the ground, never retrieving some of them. It is thus that he serves to plant our future white oak groves. Insect life (beetles, grasshoppers, caterpillar eggs, scale insects) comprise another 23 percent of his diet, leaving only one percent for bird nestlings, eggs, mice, fish, salamanders, snails, frogs, and crustaceans, all of which are included in his fare!

Naturally, bird eggs and nestlings can only be obtained during the very seasons when the bluejays themselves are also occupied with nesting activities. A friend suggests that perhaps the jays have need at this time of the calcium and other minerals present in egg shells. He and his wife crumble chicken egg shells, mix them with grit, and offer this at their feeders during the spring season. It is popular, especially with the jays, so they hope

the offering may save some small bird eggs from the 'predators'.

Although the bluejays raise only one brood per year this procedure covers a period of six weeks from the start of nest construction to fledgling. The mother jay incubates the four to six brown-spotted, buffy eggs for 17 or 18 days. It is nearly three weeks from time of hatching until the young jays, fully feathered and looking exactly like their parents except that their tails are shorter, are ready to leave the bulky, rather messy nest which most likely was placed in a large tree about ten to fifteen feet from the ground.

Dr. William J. Long in "Wings of the Forest" gives a fascinating account of his having observed a bluejay in a unique food-gathering activity. This was on Gull Island in Moosehead Lake where he had concealed himself so as to observe the nesting gulls. During an interval when no parents were present, he watched a bluejay enter the nesting ground. The jay, of course, was in great danger of being fed to baby gulls but he warily and boldly carried out his errand which was not to obtain a baby gull or gull egg (they would have seemed huge to him) but rather, by prodding the nestlings to the point of seasickness, to persuade one of them to regurgitate what it had last been fed! The jay jobbled a bit for himself, then flew off with the remainder of the disgorged food to his own nest in a nearby spruce tree!

Dr. Long has observed that bluejays will often nest near ospreys, feeding their own young with what the ospreys drop; he reports on one jay nest that was actually incorporated into the fish hawk's structure. The ospreys and jays shared the premises peaceably, the jays making the contribution of sounding the alarm whenever Dr. Long approached the nest, causing the ospreys to fly quickly home.

Their 'thief, thief!' cry is amusing, since they themselves are accused of thievery; the bluejays seem to be self-appointed vigilantes of the wildlife community. Alert, they are the first to note the presence of a hawk, a shrike, a cat; with shrill harangue they warn the smaller wild creatures of the impending danger. John K. Terres in *Songbirds in your Garden*, tells of having personally observed the jays alerting white-throated sparrows to the presence of a prowling cat of which they had been unaware. The Terreses are convinced that the bluejays, with their raucous warnings have saved the lives of many of their small bird residents.

Whether we vote for or against the bluejays, they are here to stay. They are beautiful, and they are part of our wildlife community.

Jan. 3, 1974

ABOUT THE AUTHOR

Florence (Lemkau) Heyl was born in Linden, N.J. on Oct. 26, 1908. A graduate of Montclair (N.J.) Normal School, now Montclair State University, she taught first grade for two years. Then, drawn by the opportunity to influence young girls to love camping and the out- of-doors, she began a career with the Girl Scouts. Starting with a position with the Montclair Council, she also worked in San Diego, California, and Portland, Oregon. In 1934, she was hired as the first full time director of the Lehigh County Girl Scout Council in Allentown, Pa., and remained with them until her marriage in 1940. She took particular pride in establishing their first permanent resident camp-Camp Mosey Wood. After raising four children, she began writing a nature column, *You Can Find It Wild*, in the *Call-Chronicle* newspaper, Allentown in 1970 (now the *Morning Call*). In 1973, Florence moved with her architect husband, John, to East Boothbay, Maine. She immediately contacted the local newspapers and within months, *You Can Find It Wild* was appearing in the *Boothbay Register* and *The Lincoln County News*. Florence continued her column until she was into her nineties. At the time of this printing, she had recently celebrated her 94th birthday. In 1995, she was recognized by the Maine Media Women's Communications Contest, receiving First Place and Honorable Mention awards in the Wildlife Columnist category. One judge remarked that her prose is "evocative of Thoreau. Clearly in love with nature, she spreads her passion to all who read her column".

ABOUT THE ILLUSTRATOR

Diana Dee Taylor is an artist of natural history, born and reared in Kansas, now living in Maine. Her illustration career began in the early 1970's at the *Maine Times*, and was followed by 14 books, paintings, and the formation of Tyler Publishing. In 1989, she began to design tee shirts for Liberty Graphics, producing over 100 designs to date. D.D. enjoys seeing the shirts in a movie, on television, on the shelves of the Louvre gift shop. and signing them in Tokyo.

D.D. lives in Hallowell, Maine with her husband, Hank. She has two grown children, Zachary and Kate.

ABOUT THE PHOTOGRAPHER

Tom Fegely is a freelance writer/photographer. He can be reached via email at fegleyoutdoors@mindspring.com or write to B&T Outdoor Ent., P.O. Box 986, Cherryville, PA 18035-0986

Copies of *You Can Find It Wild* are available for $14.95 U.S. from A Silver Lining in Boothbay Harbor, Maine.

A Silver Lining
17 Townsend Ave.
PO Box 477
Boothbay Harbor, ME 04538
207.633.4103

world wide web
http://www.asilverlining.com/wild

The world is so full of wondrous things,

I think we should be happy as kings.

—Unknown